DAVID MACH

DAVID MACH
LIKENESS GUARANTEED

AD ACADEMY EDITIONS
In collaboration with Newlyn Art Gallery

For my wife, Lesley, with love.

This publication is the result of a collaboration between Newlyn Art Gallery and the Academy Group. We would like to thank Emily Ash, Director of Newlyn Art Gallery for initiating the project. Thanks are also due to David and Lesley Mach for their great enthusiasm and hard work, Cairney Down for her commitment and work on this project as well as Paul Bonaventura and Tim Marlow for their written contributions.

David Mach: Likeness Guaranteed has been produced to coincide with a touring exhibition initiated by Newlyn Art Gallery which includes the sculpture *Likeness Guaranteed* (commissioned by Newlyn Art Gallery in association with Aberdeen Art Gallery, the Mercer Art Gallery, Harrogate, and the artist), and was made possible by the generous support of: The Arts Council of England; The Henry Moore Foundation; The Elephant Trust; South West Arts; Cornwall County Council.

Photographic Credits: Ace Contemporary Exhibitions pp14 (below); 70 (right), 71 (left, centre), 82 (right), 83, 84 (left, right), 85; Arts Council p10; Barbara Toll Fine Art, New York, p33 (inset, left); Bob Berry pp2, 62-67, 112-113; Jean-Luc Brutsch pp106-109; John Christie pp88-89; Ant Critchfield pp16, 18, 20, 26-29, 46-49, 30-31, 69, 70 (centre), 88-89, 90-97, 100-105, 110-111, 122-123, 124-125; Ant Critchfield and Lloyd Smith pp114-119; Mike Davis p8 (above left and right); Ron Diamond pp40-41; Fotostudio Liesl Biber pp32-33 (main image); Galérie Andata/ Ritorno, Geneva, pp68, 70(left), 98-99; Don Hall pp34-35; Bob Jardine pp42-43; Lisson Gallery, London, p12 (above); Maurice Keitelman pp74-79; Gary Kirkham pp52-55; Andrea Martiradonna pp50-51; Helmut Maurer p33 (inset, right); Musée León Dierx, Réunion Island, pp60-61; Museum of Modern Art, Oxford pp12, 14 (above); Philipp Scholz Ritterman (courtesy of the Museum of Contemporary Art, San Diego) pp58-59; Provinciaal Museum, Hasselt, pp38-39; Tate Gallery Photo Department, London, pp72-73; William Jackson Gallery, London, pp80-81, 84 (centre); Edward Woodman pp24-25; Alan Wylie pp44-45; Zindman/Fremont pp36-37, 71 (right), 82 (left, centre).

Cover: Likeness Guaranteed, 1994 (photo: Bob Berry)
Page 2: David Mach during the creation of *Temple at Tyre*, Leith Docks, Edinburgh, November 1994 (photo: Lloyd Smith)

ART & DESIGN Monograph

First published in Great Britain in 1995 by
ACADEMY EDITIONS

An imprint of
ACADEMY GROUP LTD
42 Leinster Gardens
London W2 3AN

A member of the VCH Publishing Group

ISBN 1 85490 350 0

Distributed to the trade in the United States of America by
ST MARTIN'S PRESS 175 Fifth Avenue, New York, NY 10010

Printed and bound in Singapore

CONTENTS

INTRODUCTION

Scottish born David Mach rose to prominence in the early eighties with his remarkable large-scale sculpture projects, notably *Polaris*, the submarine made entirely from tyres exhibited at the South Bank Centre in London, and his vast magazine sculptures such as *Fuel For The Fire* at the Riverside Studios in London. He has cultivated an international reputation with projects in art galleries and museums throughout the world, while also choosing to present work in a variety of more unusual locations such as swimming baths, shopping malls, parks and gardens. The often monumental proportions of his pieces together with an original choice of materials, his highly crafted technique of working and the accessibility of many of the locations where his sculptures have been sited have ensured Mach's popular status.

In May 1994, Newlyn Art Gallery re-opened following a major internal refurbishment project. David Mach was chosen to launch the artistic programme, with a show entitled 'Likeness Guaranteed', reinforcing the gallery's commitment to initiating exhibitions by major contemporary artists.

Mach's sculpture is characterised by his repeated use of multiple components such as magazines, newspapers, car tyres, bottles, matches and barbie dolls, suggesting something of today's obsession with consumerism and the subsequent level of waste it produces. His work is not created from worn-out or second hand throwaway materials but from those manufactured surplus to requirement which he radically subverts and re-invents to form something 'new'.

Likeness Guaranteed was the centrepiece of the Newlyn Art Gallery exhibition, a sculpture created from thousands of manipulated, moulded and welded metal coat hangers. Reminiscent of classical statues, this magnificent bust stood 8 feet above the floor, warrior-like, proud and imposing, as if clad in body armour and breastplates. It is in fact a portrait, conceived in a traditional manner of modelled representation. It is Mach's material and method which make this portrait unique and infuse it with contemporary references.

White Water, Yellow Splash, Red Dash which was also made for Newlyn Art Gallery typifies Mach's working practice in terms of material and response to place. Magazines and newspapers have been one of his most utilised raw materials over the past ten years, quite often between 10 and 30 tonnes at a time. Layer upon layer have formed engulfing strata of voluminous scale which have enveloped and swept along in torrents objects as large as full-scale lorries, cars, furniture, grand pianos, columns and fireplaces. Newlyn Art Gallery is positioned on the coast of Cornwall and this site-specific newspaper installation appeared to have burst through the sea-facing wall of the space. Like a surging wave it crashed into the gallery bringing with it yellow and red canoes, precariously positioned to further reinforce the illusion of undulating movement. This book provides an insight into Mach's career to date. It examines specific areas of his working practice and looks in detail at some of the major pieces that have brought him such wide critical and popular acclaim.

Emily Ash, Director of Newlyn Art Gallery

White Water, Yellow Splash, Red Dash,
Newlyn Art Gallery, Cornwall, April 1994

From above L to R: Alyth Sawmill, *Alyth, 1977;* Camperdown Park, *Dundee, 1978;* Running Out of Steam, *Royal College of Art Degree Show, London, 1982;* Silver Cloud III, *Hay-on-Wye, 1981 (later exhibited at Royal College of Art Degree Show)*

Thinking Big
PAUL BONAVENTURA

NEWS INTERNATIONAL

In 1985 Keynote Publications produced an industry sector overview of the state of consumer magazines in Great Britain and Northern Ireland.[1] Excluding those titles targeted specifically at women and the business community, the number of periodicals available to the buying public had almost doubled in the previous twenty years from 820 in 1963 to a figure approaching 1,600 in 1984. If the number of start-ups and failures had also been taken into consideration that final count would have run into many thousands. The report confirmed the importance of advertising to the business of publishing and stated that over the previous decade the industry had been dominated by the Independent Publishing Corporation, a subsidiary of the diversified British-based conglomerate Reed International. Ten years ago, IPC probably sold or distributed 236 million magazines annually, roughly 16 per cent of the total estimated annual inland sales of 1,500 million.

By the mid-1980s almost every category of consumer magazine had seen an increase in the number of titles assigned to it. Correspondingly, circulation figures showed that most publications had lost sales, partly because people were buying fewer magazines, but mainly because there were so many to choose from in each sector that even long-established titles had been encountering fierce competition on the newsstand. It was against this background, a background dominated by commerce, publicity, profitability and overproduction, that the Scottish-born sculptor David Mach turned his attention to the creative potential presented by magazines as an appropriate subject for his work.

In the space occupied by the arts and media, periodicals run television a close second as the pre-eminent carrier of meaning in our time. You do not have to be familiar with the languages and contents of consumer magazines globally to understand and appreciate their functions, to comprehend the appealing consensus of opinion offered up by publishers in Paris, Perth and Pretoria. Magazines provide their readers with up-to-the-minute information on a seemingly infinite range of topics and bring happenings and events of lasting historical significance into millions of front rooms all over the world. Reading about or seeing something in a magazine provides an experience akin to being there and witnessing it in person.

Notwithstanding the pattern of fluctuating fortunes which continue to beset the publications industry, the colourful layout and lush imagery, the shiny texture, and even the smell of the printed page ensure that magazines will never completely lose their fascination. Added to the sense of pleasure associated with the very act of reading itself is the sought-after attractiveness of magazines as cultural objects in their own right. In purchasing magazines we buy into a sense of community, taking out shares in the commodified worlds of 'make-believe' which magazines relentlessly espouse, inviting worlds where desire and consumerism have become largely indistinguishable. The messages contained in the images, features and regular columns are closely allied with the promotion of certain goods and services and reveal the crucial role played by advertising in the shaping of style and content.[2]

Front covers, whose ostensible function it is to promote the editorial material to be found inside, are in fact magazines' most important advertisements, the labels without which readers might not come across the other promotions elsewhere. In some instances, David Mach has allowed the covers of his component magazines the metaphorical as well as the literal space in which to contribute to the overall meaning of his work. His model rendition of half of *La Tour Eiffel*, for example, which occupied a corner of his Royal College of Art Degree Show in London in 1982, was constructed out of copies of the *Time Out Guide to Paris*, underlining the sense of place already present in the sculpture. Less obviously, but perhaps more trenchantly, the way in which the artist utilised thousands of copies of a pornographic magazine later in the same year for *Silent Running* reinforced the sexual connotations aroused by his portrayal of a nuclear submarine surfacing through the floor of the Galerie t'Venster in Rotterdam.

Because of its scale, Mach's work with magazines and other printed items frequently requires considerable financial support, not least in the form of in-kind sponsorship from publishers and wholesalers. Although we as spectators may feel a little uneasy at the overt intrusion of business into what is usually regarded as the rarefied domain inhabited by the arts, the artist himself adopts an altogether different stance and is only too happy to acknowledge his backers either on the work itself or in the accompanying documentation: 'I know from being in this world,' comments Mach, 'that people are very funny about advertising. They seem to think that the work is somehow tainted by it. But for me, working with advertising is an attempt to exist in the real world as an artist.'[3] Commerce, for Mach, is not just a means to an end. It is an essential element in the content of his sculpture, one which takes its lead from the magazine industry itself. If the other lives of his raw materials were somehow disguised or ignored, the impact of

the work and the web-like complexity of meanings which both surround and inform it would be correspondingly reduced.

Thirteen years on from his Royal College show, the exhibition at which most spectators got their first glimpse of his magazine- and book-based replicas of objects, Mach's work with printed matter continues to pile up and it is with these pieces in particular that he has become most closely identified. Organised in huge layered stacks, tens of tonnes at a time, magazines provide the artist with an eminently pliant and value-laden medium, the expressive possibilities of which the artist has managed to harness in remarkably diverse ways:

> With magazines, I find that I can achieve a great variety of results, depending on the size, weight and texture of the paper from which they are made and, of course, the contents. Also, I find that when I combine the magazines with other materials, other objects, new ways of working are revealed. The materials carry with them these extraordinary messages and it's my job as an artist to deliver those up.

The ways in which the sculptor has extracted those messages, from newspapers and directories as well as magazines and books, can be divided into two closely-related groups of work. Up until 1985, Mach worked representationally using the extravagant surpluses associated with mass production to create instantly recognisable likenesses of existing things. These included automobiles (*Silver Cloud III* of 1981 and *Volkswagen* of 1982), a locomotive (*Running Out of Steam*), a tank (*Centurion Tank*), figures (*Reclining Figure* and *Reclining Nude*) and a felled tree (*Palm Down*) all of 1982, as well as a submarine and a public monument. Over the past decade, Mach has mostly employed printed matter in the creation of something rather more allegorical, a product of his increasing familiarity with the liquid-like properties of glossy journals and their apparently seamless and indiscriminate treatment of local, national and international news.[4] Nowadays, Mach's magazine mountains are variously charmed and cajoled into depictions of smoke, water or lava, fluid fields within whose vortices real things have been swept up and carried away. Coming in the wake of his earlier facsimiles, these washed-away objects might almost be looked upon as 'inverse surrogates' which have somehow been given licence to deputise for items reproduced within the pages of the magazines themselves.

The first of these structures, for the Galerie Foksal in Warsaw in 1985, focused on a small magazine-based hearth. One year later, *Fuel for the Fire* was allowed to engulf the entire gallery at the Riverside Studios in London and set in train a number of projects including *Outside In* and *Adding Fuel to the Fire*, both of 1987, *A Million Miles Away* of 1988 and, just last year, *White Water, Yellow Splash, Red Dash* at Newlyn Art Gallery. Notwithstanding the generic similarity between them, these sculptures encompass an approach to making and thinking about the world which continues to inspire the artist's creative imagination fully ten years after their initial manifestation:

Polaris, *South Bank Centre, London, 1983*

You begin by contemplating a swirl of smoke, but soon start thinking about less obvious parallels: water, hair, rock strata. Because I am involved with the process of paring things down to their essential forms, I concern myself with only capturing the most important elements of any given motif.[5]

Fuel for the Fire marked a turning point in Mach's work with magazines. The half-submerged objects which he was obliged to negotiate in putting up his sculptures began functioning like boulders in a stream, so much so that Mach felt he was drawing around them, redescribing their salient features in negative. Suddenly, he realised that the magazines themselves had started to dictate how the pieces were developing:

> They began to do their own thing, heading off in unlooked-for directions and telling me what sort of forms I should make.
> I found that the materials had their own energy, their own flow. It's a bit like dealing with the grain in a piece of stone or wood . . . That energy source is a very abstract idea.[6]

To hear somebody like Mach, the arch-maker of objects, referring to abstract ideas might, at first, sound rather strange. At source, however, the will to recreate things from quotidian reality derives from the need in all of us to make sense of the complexities of life on our own terms. When we call up images from our memories, they most often appear before the mind's eye in something approaching their ideal form and it is in this way that they are most efficiently remembered. As we indulge our desire to configure the world in our own likeness, the impulse to simplify and make manageable figures large.

MULTIPLE CHOICE

David Mach was born in Methil, Fife on 18 March 1956 to a Polish father and a Scottish mother. He graduated from Duncan Jordanstone College of Art in Dundee in 1979 with first class honours before moving to London to enrol as a postgraduate at the Royal College. During the course of his studies as a student artist both in Scotland and England, Mach supplemented his basic grant by spending periods of time as a labourer on building sites and as an unskilled worker on the factory floor. His experiences in a bottling plant and in companies which manufactured telegraph poles, racking systems for whisky barrels and canned foodstuffs were at least as important as his studio activities in defining the future direction of his work. For it was while he was undertaking these banal and mind-numbing activities that Mach came to understand the value of working with multiples of certain basic units, a principle he has applied inventively and to flamboyant and spectacular effect ever since.

Inevitably for most observers, Mach has come to be associated with that group of British sculptors which came to prominence in the early 1980s, linked as they were by their use of obsolete or superfluous manufactured objects. Tony Cragg and Bill Woodrow, in particular, adopted methods of assemblage which developed and sometimes embellished the original identities of the second-hand or thrown-away implements selected for use, fostering comparisons with the ways in which Pop artists and, before them, the Surrealists had regarded and intervened in the space of lived experience. Mach, by contrast, works in ways which usually leave his accessories 'as new'. Tyres, bottles, postcards, plates, lamps, coat hangers, freight containers, matchsticks, publications, shoes, children's toys, stuffed animals, games, advertisements and a dizzying array of consumer durables have all, at times, been commandeered by the artist and transformed with a clear-cut economy of means into the most extraordinary sculptures. Perceived immediately as being of their own time, many of these mass-produced items occupy a hybrid zone somewhere between fine art, architecture and design. In searching for new ideas, Mach has allowed his imagination free-range over different disciplines and materials and shudders at the prospect of being tied down in the development of his practice:

> Why should you have to ditch nine ideas in order to realise a tenth? I'd rather deal with all ten at once even if that causes me problems.

Indisputably, David Mach likes to think big:

> You want your work to have this enormous effect. You want people to write about it, to applaud it, love it, buy it even! But all you can normally expect is the opposite. There are millions of people out there just waiting to ignore me so I have to keep leaping up and down shouting: 'Yoo-hoo. Come and have a look at this.'

The practical problems which this approach generates can often be formidable and the artist has frequently had to adapt his initial plans during the process of construction in order to accommodate the structural limitations inherent in his chosen media, the number of assistants made available to him on any one project, deadlines and other logistical considerations.

The ways in which Mach has used manufactured objects over the past decade and a half can be traced back to his earlier manipulation of offcuts of wood and fallen leaves as an undergraduate.[7] In his five years as a student at Duncan of Jordanstone College, he found that his most satisfying experiments were always conducted away from the preciousness of the studio and all of the expectations that went with it. *Alyth Sawmill* of 1977 and *Camperdown Park* of 1978, the two works which first provide evidence of his subsequent preoccupations, comprised stacked and layered strips of timber and leaves woven into eye-catching repeat-pattern structures. The experience of making sculpture in the woodyards and woodlands around Dundee revealed to Mach that if his art was to stand any chance of competing with the richness of the natural and man-made environments from which it derived then it was going to have to signal its presence in a brash and demonstrative fashion.

Although he would hate to be regarded as a populist, Mach steadfastly believes that artists should set out to attract wide-ranging support for their work without descending to the level of

11

From above: Reclining Nude, *Lisson Gallery, London, 1982;* Foxtrot, *Museum of Modern Art, Oxford, 1985*

the lowest common denominator. As a consequence, he is only too happy to avail himself of the seductive properties of the dramatic and the absurd in beguiling audiences which might not otherwise take an interest in the work. In courting a non-museum-going following, Mach resents the accusation that his work lacks gravity:

Artists do not have problems with the seriousness of their work. It's other people that do that: the politicians, the curators and the critics. And yet all the time you're running scared because you're wondering whether sometimes you might be going too far and exhibiting opportunities are going to dry up . . . The only thing you can do is be honest with yourself and be consistent in that honesty. Inevitably, you'll end up shooting yourself in the foot a hundred times a week, but that's the price you have to pay.

Possibly more than any other artist in Britain today, Mach's sculptures have regularly become the subject of modern myth.[8] His *Polaris*, a one-half scale rubber-tyre replica of a nuclear submarine for 'British Sculpture 83' at the Hayward Gallery in London, generated a political controversy even before it was destroyed in an act of needless vandalism. Likewise, the twin themes of nationalism and sexism explored in *Thinking of England* of 1983 and *Dying for It* of 1989 have occasionally served to attract garbled and misplaced commentary. Nevertheless, Mach is still looking to make his mark on the world and continues to chart the margins, entering into commercial ventures with magazine publishers, national and regional television channels and the music industry. Some of these projects have been more successful than others, but all have been conspicuous, assuring Mach a regular dose of high-profile exposure and an opportunity to mine new and sometimes unexpected outlets.

In keeping with the magazine and book installations, the coat hanger, tyre, bottle, postcard, match and plate pieces are similarly tiered and emphasise the fact that the sculptor's way of working has remained remarkably consistent throughout his career. Forerunners of the recent coat hanger busts, the match heads can trace their lineage back to Mach's 1982 portrait of the German film star Klaus Kinski as he appeared in the feature film *Burden of Dreams*. These structures, contemporary versions of ancient theatrical, ceremonial or armoured masks, throw up immediate parallels with the craft-based activities of hobbyists, those who spend their Sunday afternoons hidden away in garden sheds on replicas of Durham Cathedral and the Ark Royal. Each piece can take up to a month to fabricate and Mach, in partnership with his wife Lesley, uses both ends of the match to generate a decorative and sometimes startling polychromy. The multicoloured physiognomies of some of the heads generate associations with the look of faces depicted in more radical magazine-based promotions for female cosmetics. By the same token, other heads foment a correspondence with the pronounced facial markings employed for a variety of social purposes by diverse non-Western cultures. In this respect, some of the most recent masks, derived from historic African examples seen by Mach on a visit to the island of Réunion off Madagascar, might almost read as the beginnings of some kind of programmatic taxonomic investigation into the evolution of face-painting as a vehicle for non-verbal communication.

Mach realises that he is taking liberties in this body of work with a rich and complex tradition other than his own. He has pushed things just about as far as they can go by depicting some of the heads in the act of consuming children's toys, the very same figures which he had previously pressed into service as caryatids in pieces such as *If You go Down to the Woods Today* of 1987 and *Off the Beaten Track* of 1988. As well as alluding to the process and function of recycling, the munching heads might be seen as passing comment on the sometimes painful metamorphosis which manifests itself in adolescence as childhood merges into adulthood, a transformation which finds like-symbolic form when the busts themselves are actually set ablaze. Allowed to burn ferociously for a few seconds, the match heads are then extinguished which not only preserves a ghost-like tracery of the original facial patterning, but also encourages ritualistic readings: rites-of-passage, fertility rituals, devil worship – what the artist likes to think of as creepy, superstitious stuff. Mach enjoys the opportunities to perform which these pyrotechnic displays provide and frequently arranges it so that the burnings take place in public, either at exhibition openings or in front of family and friends, holding the incandescent forms aloft in an asbestos-gloved hand or on a suitably long pole.

To some extent, all of Mach's sculptural brandishments might be regarded as the residue of performances, a sublimated instinct on the part of the artist to play-act. In the past, Mach has appeared in reproductions taken during the course of installations, most conspicuously in the catalogues which accompanied *Fuel for the Fire* of 1986 and *Between the Lines* of 1993. Although these narratives function as documentaries, charting the progress of a work from birth to completion, they also reveal at work a showman, someone who positively relishes the cut and thrust precipitated by being on display during the making of a sculpture. The unremitting routines by which his building-scale forms come to life, captured as film stills, have all the hallmarks of a dance and point to yet another means of attracting audiences which might otherwise be less than enthusiastic about involving themselves in the seemingly hermetic world of contemporary art.

The direction in which Mach's work is travelling during the course of an installation is never affected by his exchanges with onlookers, those who just happen to drop by while a piece is under construction, although ideas generated in conversation with visitors have frequently found an outlet in subsequent sculptures. For Mach, these discussions galvanise the work and convert the history of its making into something more dynamic and resonant. In part, the presence of the public also offsets the long hours of tedium engendered in his working practice:

Audiences have the ability to make the smallest details fascinating for me, to make me look again at actions which I might not have thought about closely for years. Ironically, if someone's watching me knocking in a nail, it helps me to concentrate more fully. It's not a distraction.

The dialogues which intervene in the making and presentation of work embrace real-life issues, matters which are never far from the surface of Mach's artistic endeavours. Instead of becoming irritated by them, the sculptor welcomes their intrusion and senses that they prevent his work from becoming too obtuse, too arcane. Mach regards the kind of art that fulfils only a decorative role as a worthless luxury, a position which possibly finds its source in the working class industrial background into which he was born. Moreover, he never underestimates the imaginative resources of his audiences and hugely enjoys exhibiting in all sorts of spaces – discotheques, shopping centres, car parks, municipal parks, trains, swimming pools, fountains, dockyards – spaces, that is, other than those provided for by museums and galleries:

These places have been really great for me artistically. For my practice, for my heart, for my wallet! So what is it that I'm not getting from working all the time in other more distinguished settings?

Even while he was at Dundee, Mach was becoming increasingly disenchanted with the concept of working in college, representing as it did an environment from which he was already drawing back. This withdrawal from the world of artful interiors found its most extreme exposure in the Edwardian trophy room erected as part of his mid-career retrospective at The Centre for Contemporary Art in Warsaw in 1993.[9] The Centre occupies the old Ujazdowski Castle, a benign and dream-like fortification on the outskirts of the city. At the time of Mach's exhibition, the Castle was in the throes of a major refurbishment in which individual rooms were being converted into the clean white cubes of a modern art museum. Perversely, Mach decided that he wanted to re-introduce into the building a full-blown baronial interior, complete with wood panelling, leather furniture, red carpeting, wall trophies and a full-size snooker table, a setting, in short, which looked at home in a citadel.

The idea behind *The Trophy Room* stemmed originally from Mach's musings on the exclusivity of the art world and on how individuals are either made to feel welcome or ignored by that establishment. What better analogy for a society of members and non-members than a gentleman's club? What more appropriate symbol of belonging than the commemorative 'bang-it-stuff-it-set-it-up' wall trophy? In contradistinction to traditional souvenirs, Mach's score of 'double-trophies' brought together a variety of stuffed animal heads with items from the well-appointed home. The boar with the running machine (*Hot to Trot*), the lion with the motor bike (*King of the Road*) and the otter with the smart log-effect convection heater (*Mistaken Identity*) are the direct descendents of a series of bronze and fibreglass gargoyles on

13

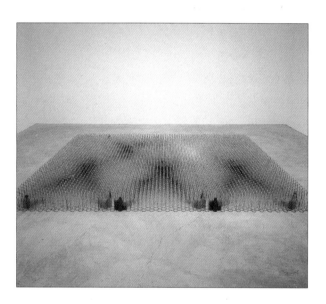

From above: Knuckle Shuffle, *Museum of Modern Art, Oxford, 1985;* There Wasn't Much Room in the Pool for Individual Expression (Especially if you're a Woman), *Ace Contemporary Exhibitions, Los Angeles, 1991*

which the artist first began working in 1987.[10] These are the perversely-coupled rewards of money and position, the creature comforts to which we all aspire. These are the tokens by which we measure our status and success.

WIRED UP

Ambition is the motive force which propels David Mach towards working on a larger and larger scale, towards making things grander, evermore unforgettable. The last thing he wants is for his work to be easy, either to assimilate or to make. The freight container sculptures, such as the sumo-wrestling *It Takes Two*, raise the requirement for practical problem-solving onto another level entirely: 'A container is like a fantastic building block, a huge plinth, a minimal work of art in its own right. At the same time, it represents all of the goods transported within it. Fabulous, but it's a hell of a thing to deal with!' Originally created as *Over to the Right a Bit* for an exhibition in Kiev in 1989 as a comment on a society in flux, the wrestlers were modelled in a half-Disney-half-Socialist-Realist manner in response to the thrusting statues of Lenin which Mach had seen on a previous visit to the Soviet Union. Ironically, the idea for working with giant containers came while he was labouring on the much smaller match heads. With their rigorously columnar profiles, the backsides of the human-sized heads provoked Mach into thinking about the basalt-columned Giant's Causeway and ultimately provided the stimulus for a whole series of projects taking in the girder head for the M8 Art Project in Scotland, a recently-unveiled container and rubber tyre version of the Parthenon on the Acropolis in Leith called *Temple at Tyre*,[11] and a proposal for an as yet unrealised Valley of the Kings-style sculpture park for Motherwell.

Mach questions the value of the term 'site-specific' when it applies to art in public, sensing that the demands made by commissioners come close in their requirements to those made by advertisers:

I believe absolutely in the merits of wherever I happen to be working and take on as many of the physical, social, material, image-based and process-based concerns as I can. But once you arrive at a dozen separate preconditions for a location, you start to lose count. I feel that a piece is deficient if it cannot be lifted up and taken to be seen some place else.

In the case of the sculptures which utilise freight containers, the specificity comes not from the image created, but from the components themselves. Containers, like magazines, function as international currency and confer on the works in which they are used a universal pertinence.

All of the components which Mach uses in his work have about them an agreeable accessibility. Plates, bottles, tyres and magazines perform easily-comprehensible functions and are immediately suggestive of a human agency. But perhaps nothing that the artist has used to date more obviously evokes the human figure than the coat hanger, a shaped piece of steel which stands in for the missing body, both clothed and naked. The first essay in his newly-metallic exploration of portraiture, *Wire Head* of 1992, is an effigy of the artist's brother and hangs from the wall. The two much larger freestanding pieces, blow-ups of neoclassical or imperial busts, are depicted on plinths or sculpted bases. *Likeness Guaranteed*, a portrait of television presenter and ex-singer of The Skids Richard Jobson, and *Wired*, a portrait of Hugh Cornwall of The Stranglers, both of 1993, exist within silvery-hooked haloes of their own making and have an obviously drawn quality to them, not unlike three-dimensional silver points.[12]

For *Likeness Guaranteed*, commissioned by Newlyn Art Gallery for its eponymous exhibition in 1994, Mach chose Jobson as his subject because of his 'chiselled good looks' and because today's heroes come not from politics and literature, but from the worlds of pop and rock music, from television and the cinema. Singers and television presenters represent figures who have re-invented themselves for public consumption; as for Jobson, so for Cornwall. In allowing the hangers to retain their hooked ends, the artist has created a pair of brittle-looking portraits in cages. Calling to mind the similarly swirling forms in his flows of magazines, the eddying mass of spiky extrusions prevent us from inspecting these portraits too closely, just in case their pasts are too unpalatable, their re-inventions less than perfect. Like trophies, statues are steeped in their own histories, some more acceptable than others.

After all else, perhaps the best way to comprehend the work of David Mach is to think of it as a provocation. In creating likenesses of things from multiple units of everyday objects, Mach sets the world which we make for ourselves against itself and uses the opportunity to draw our attention to the wastefulness which is so much a part of our customary lives. Despite the waggishness endemic to his approach, we would do well to bear in mind the seriousness of the issues which the sculptor's work addresses. As Simon Anderson has noted, Mach's multitudes might 'seem excessive, even obscene [yet] he uses amounts which are puny in comparison to the number of objects which clutter our daily ritual of buying, fantasising and fetishism.'[13] So the next time you make a trip to the newsagents, take another look at those serried ranks of seductively-packaged magazines festooning the walls and ask yourself: 'Do we really need so many things in our lives to render them affable? Do we really need so much identical and trivial information to be secure of our place in the world?'

For Jane Sackville West

Paul Bonaventura is Erna Plachte Senior Research Fellow in Fine Art Studies at the Ruskin School of Drawing and Fine Art, Oxford University.

Footnotes

1 *Consumer Magazines: An Industry Sector Overview*, Keynote Publications Ltd (London) 1985.

2 This information on magazines as mass cultural forms has been taken from *Decoding Women's Magazines: From Mademoiselle to Ms*, Ellen McCracken, The Macmillan Press Ltd (Basingstoke and London) 1993.

3 From an unpublished conversation with the author which took place at the artist's home on 30 June and 1 July 1994. Unless otherwise specified, all quotations by David Mach are from this source.

4 The only object-based structures which have in any real sense persisted beyond the mid-1980s are the magazine columns such as *Here to Stay* of 1990 and *Between the Lines* of 1993. Ordinarily, architectural columns have structural functions. Mach's columns have little load-bearing capacity and appear vaguely incongruous in their largely modern settings. In juxtaposing the classical against the contemporary, and in some instances the contemporary industrial, Mach is possibly suggesting that the capacity to bear weight in a given space – physical, environmental, social – is as much emblematic as it is earthly and that impressions of strength may be misleading.

5 'Not Necessarily Representational: David Mach Interviewed', *Artefactum*, Spring 1987, vol 3, no 16, pp17-21.

6 Ibid.

7 For a thorough introduction to Mach's early work, see Marco Livingstone's essay in *David Mach: Towards a Landscape*, Museum of Modern Art (Oxford) 1985.

8 It might be argued that Damien Hirst also has claims in this area.

9 The exhibition was made the subject of a short film entitled *From Hill to Castle*, produced by Annalogue Productions for BBC Scotland and the Arts Council of Great Britain. The programme was broadcast as an item on BBC 2's *The Late Show* and provided a digest of many of the themes, interests and concerns which characterise Mach's work

10 The title *Mistaken Identity* suggested itself to Mach after he realised that what he had originally thought to be a stuffed beaver's head was in fact a stuffed otter's head.

11 *Temple at Tyre* was commissioned by the Bid Partners for Edinburgh as Capital of Architecture and Design in 1999, part of the Arts Council of England's Millennium Project.

12 A technique of drawing on paper with a piece of silver wire held in wood like graphite in a modern pencil. The point produces a silvery-grey line which is indelible and therefore encourages the maker to think carefully before making a mark

13 *Secco y Mojado: Wet and Dry*, Centro Cultural de la Villa and the British Council (Madrid) 1989.

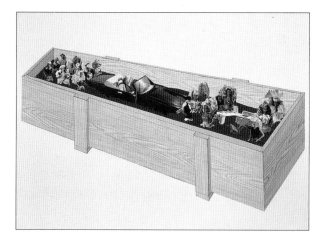

Above: The Devil You Know, *1992, drawings for a proposed statue of Lenin which was to shower gifts on the people of Warsaw when smashed; Below:* Barbie Army, *1992 (both unrealised)*

DAVID MACH
AN INTERVIEW WITH TIM MARLOW

TM: Art historians and critics are much more obsessed with categories than artists are but after fifteen years do you have a way of categorising your own work, of breaking it down into certain areas?

DM: Only in a very loose way. Take the piece I've been working on in Darlington. It's a huge public piece of work, a train made out of bricks which envelopes itself in its own steam also made out of bricks. The steam turns into a row of terraced houses going uphill so eventually you get less and less steam – and more and more house until you have a complete house in which someone could actually live. It's a big project and a huge landmass is involved in it, you're talking about using diggers and other big pieces of machinery, never mind the size of the team to put it together. Then I switch from that to a gallery and maybe I'm showing tiny match-made pieces or a series of parthenons or temples made of toy tyres. Then again it could be another big project. We've just completed one in Edinburgh where there's a parthenon on top of 140 metal sea-cargo containers. I like jumping around like that and while those things don't defy being categorised they don't necessarily encourage it either. Maybe it's not a great help for me to categorise. Maybe that's when I feel pinned down.

TM: Is that how you work creatively – with ideas and objects constantly fuelling and feeding into the work without you ever having to stop, take stock and think about new directions?

DM: Well they're all new directions in a sense. It's a constant journey or search. I'm trying to think of a less poncy way of putting it. You don't stop, it's an ongoing thing. You wake up thinking about it, you go to bed thinking about it, you're jogging in the park thinking about it. I look at things all the time wondering how I can use this or that, not just for sculpture, maybe I'm looking for a new idea for a towel rail or maybe it's a wall surface. It depends if I'm thinking about a particular job or just letting my mind wander.

TM: If it is a journey, do you have an idea of what it is, ultimately, that you are seeking?

DM: I don't think there is an end to a journey like this. I certainly don't want there to be an end. I want to get to be an ancient old decrepit who can't stop, and hopefully who hasn't run out of ideas either. It's just a continuous thing. Why should there be an end to

it, a goal? I don't think about it in those terms at all. There are things to be done and I think, 'well, let's just do it'. And when it's done there's a real buzz. I was thrilled to bits that we managed to build something as big as the classical temple in Edinburgh. It's over 80 feet tall and I would hope that it's going to be one of the smallest things that we do in the next ten years.

TM: Why this obsession with getting big?

DM: It's to do with excess. I love the idea of being excessive with art, making huge statements, grand gestures.

TM: Your work is often perceived in terms of the culture of excess or waste. But do you want to make social or political points? During recession, I don't see you in any way cutting back on your materials, you're getting larger. Is this irony or 'up yours'?

DM: Much more than 'up yours'. It's to do with this country and its conservative nature. How do you deal with recessions . . . you tighten your belt, suck everything in, narrow it down, make more sense of it, make financial sense. Why do we have to do that? Let's not do that, let's go the other way.

That's one of the reasons we get in such a mess. We have recessions because we don't encourage the very guys who have ideas. Ultimately if you don't have artists you don't even have door handles or at best you get lousy door handles nobody wants to buy. I think art can have a firm, hard effect on industry like that. It's not just art for art's sake and people's souls and all that sort of stuff. It goes right into the heart of industry and ends up putting money in people's pockets. It's a seed, it actually feeds those kinds of things.

TM: How do you feed directly into industry?

DM: You feed it with ideas. Pure design doesn't exist any more. It's been cut back and over-rationalised in art schools and totally geared towards mass production to the extent that ideas are a poor second to making or rather saving money. Artists are deal- ing with ideas and how to make them tangible the whole time and generate all sorts of possibilities. Industry can take some of those possibilities as they are or hammer them out even more. Either way, art is influential, but it is not an easy thing to prove. You can't often say this artist made this, the knock-on effect is that and

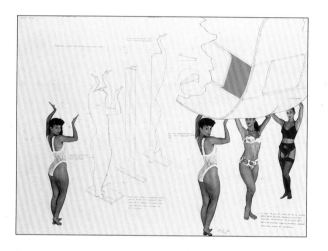

From above: Drawing for Jeep and Charity Figures, *1992; proposal for Venice Biennale sculpture, 1989 (both unrealised)*

they, industry, made this much money and everybody ran off and was happy. But I believe that that's actually how it works.

T M : So you think that innovation and originality are central tenets of art and that's still what it's all about?

D M : Yes. To me that's what it's still about.

T M : Your conception of an artist, your projection of yourself as an artist is diametrically opposed to the romantic idea of the lonely figure tucked away in a garret. You operate in the public domain. Could you ever see yourself disappearing off for a few years to work in a studio?

D M :I don't see it happening now. It's much better for me to be with people in a busy place. It might not necessarily be a ready-made place in which to make art because people are already on the attack where you're involved in a much more aggressive act, but I find it very stimulating. This romantic idea of an artist slowly working out ideas in his studio still seems to have an appeal and a lot of people make work like that. I don't want to slag it off but I just can't work like that. I'd dry up.

T M : Do you draw?

D M : Yes, but I don't sketch ideas in order to be able to make work. I get involved in all these public projects where you can't just walk in and talk about something. You've got to show them something more concrete, so I spend a fair bit of time working on things like that, to show them 'this is what it might look like'.

T M : How clear an idea do you have of the larger-scale public projects before they're actually made? Does the finished work correspond closely to the initial idea?

D M : It's very clear in my mind. It may not be the same as the drawing, which is why I'm rather wary of drawing it. If you do a drawing and people say, 'but I thought it was going to look like this', I have to say, 'No, I said it might look like this. This is an idea'. But in my mind I've actually got a fairly sharp idea and image.

T M : But the act of making the work and your engagement with materials is where you learn most of all?

D M : Absolutely. Say if I'm working with magazines. I can sit down and do a drawing of a magazine piece till I am blue in the face. I could do hundreds of them but they'd never tell me one single thing, or very little about how you actually work with magazines. This is what I do every time whether I'm working with containers, tyres, magazines, Sindy dolls, or bottles. Whatever the hell it is, you're actually picking that thing up and finding out what the hell it is about. OK? So I may have an image in my head which seems really sharp but if I let that image have more importance than the actual process of working with this thing then it totally wrecks it. It's happened to me umpteen times, I'm so busy making it look absolutely like the thing in my head that I stop going with the material itself.

Magazines, for instance, are fantastic things. They have an incredible energy that is every bit as powerful as working with stone or paint or other more traditional materials. It's all in there. You've got to work with the substance of the stuff: what kind of magazine is it? Is it a porno thing? Is it a *Time Out* magazine? What's the size of the thing, the thickness of the thing, the weight of it and so on . . . American magazines you can hardly hold because they're so slidey. They're like bars of soap. So whatever images you've got in your head, you can't neglect the physical nature of the stuff you work with. It's a weird balance, but it's important to me. I don't want to be just someone who makes something out of a pile of other objects. That's not what I do. Find out how your material works and find out how that affects the image that you're making and remember your material and your image are never alone.

The project in Edinburgh took a month of working with half a dozen Geordies abseiling up and down it. We had a strict time limit, there was the weather to consider and so on. All sorts of things you'll never find out in a studio. So there's a performance element perhaps, which is the main ingredient of how you mix those things together: your process, your materials, your image, your site, whether that site is an art place, whether it's an art gallery or in a sculpture park, whether it's in a supermarket or wherever, all those things have an effect. It's impossible to ignore them.

TM: How can art galleries ever excite you to create when you've got the whole world, potentially, in which to build your sculpture?

DM: Well, art galleries have an audience that I want to reach. That's where a lot of people start off with art. And that's where you can begin to open their minds.

TM: So you are an artist with a mission? You want to spread the word?

DM: Well it's not a religion. I don't feel like a zealot, a newly baptised minister out there spreading the word. It's one thing that pisses me off about galleries, they do tend to preach to the converted. You know, they become little style clubs, even big museums, but there's a valid audience there and it'd be stupid of me to say 'I'm never going to show in art galleries because they're full of poncy people who like art'. I want to show my work to everybody. I want people to like it, I want people to love it, I want them to be so happy they start throwing money at me, y' know? I want critics to write seriously long and boring articles about it in

all the major art magazines in the world, I want all those things, but I can't expect them. I can just show you, and then if you turn round and tell me to take a hike then, whatever, I've got to deal with that, so it's not a question of popularising.

TM: If someone does something as violent as sets fire to a work of yours – as they did with the Polaris submarine – does that in some ways thrill you because it's an extreme response?

DM: No, not really. That's happened once and only then because the guy was mentally disturbed. It didn't happen solely because he objected to what I'd done. It was a far too complicated situation to say what he really thought. If he had survived and had done it because he thought it was a heap of old rubbish then I suppose that would have been a different matter. I could have got my teeth into that.

TM: Public art is a term that has been bandied about for the last twenty-three years and it's a very problematic area, particularly in Britain, because it's inevitably associated with sculptures plonked down in sites with which they have no relationship. Are you still conscious though, of trying to develop or expand that particular tradition? Are you trying to kick that tradition about? Or are you just making sculpture in the public domain because it happens to be the most convenient place for you to make sculpture.

DM: I'm trying to kick it about but at the same time I'm trying to kick the gallery tradition about and ironically make it a public place as well. I don't think good public art is, as you imply, plonked down in the streets and it shouldn't take all the blame for contemporary art's problems. I think galleries and museums have a far bigger share of the responsibility for that and for not making what happens inside their walls 'public art'. Probably the term we should use is just 'art', we shouldn't actually have to say 'public art', it should all be bloody public. It's slightly complicated by the idea of people collecting for their own houses or corporate collections or whatever, but only slightly, the rest of it should all be in the public domain.

TM: Do you have a moral position about material? Because you recycle so much and a lot of your material is returned or it's waste material?

DM: Not really. I'm not using magazines because I'm making comments about chopping down rainforests or anything like that, it just sort of happens that those things are wrapped up with those morals, I don't think any more about it than anybody else does. It's not a moral crusade.

TM: But do you recycle material that would otherwise be waste

19

material, magazines that have been overprinted and so on, so there is a sense of the ecological . . .

DM: There's a bit of it but I also use brand new consumer goods that I can go out and buy in the shops. I'm a real nit-picker about this: 'What do you use? Do you use junk?' No, we don't use junk, newspapers, these kinds of things aren't junk, they're overproduced, perfectly good, absolutely brand new things. They may be out of date, or they may not be, they may actually be next week's, it depends, but they are not junk. 'Junk' implies to me something which has no use at all and therefore is 'a waste'. To recycle, that would be an ecological thing. However, I'm not doing that. I am not making compost for someone's tomatoes or making clothes for poor people in some Third World country or making a statement on the economic viability of these recycling processes and the resultant saving of the world's resources. I am simply talking about what these things, these objects, materials, are in the first place, and discussing how we might look at them.

We made a piece with wire coat hangers – one of the pieces in the Newlyn show – it took three months, three guys, seven days a week, twelve hours a day – £20,000 it cost to make the piece, more than that, that's just roughing it out. It's a beautiful piece called *Likeness Guaranteed* which perhaps is a bit too flippant and playful.

I won a prize with the first coat hanger piece in Glasgow, which is neither here nor there, but we got a couple of articles about it. One said, 'I am sick to death of seeing things that my five year old nephew can chuck together on a weekend'. Now whoever wrote that obviously didn't see it. The important thing to do is to go and see for yourself and then you can make decisions about it. When you go to a shop to buy something you don't run in with your money and say, 'Give me those trousers' and immediately run off. You take a little time to choose, you make decisions, whether it is something to live with, something to wear, something to drive and so on. But when it comes to art all this seems to fly out of the window, for some reason people are embarrassed or scared to make decisions about art, scared to look. That's where the real problems are.

TM: Are you getting more interested the bigger and more difficult the challenge?

DM: Not necessarily. I'm just as interested as I ever was but the projects are becoming bigger, more difficult and more challenging.

TM: But you're not interested in a one-liner that you can do just like that?

DM: You're right. Absolutely not. None of these things are ever one-liners. I really detest that. When I started making those

From above: Proposal for sculpture in Musée Léon Dierx, Réunion Island, 1993; Heavenly Pursuits, 1992 (both unrealised)

magazine pieces I used to really worry about that. I made a small submarine with magazines, I made a Rolls Royce out of books, I made a train and so on. In fact, I made about six pieces and I had about twenty shows and then I gave it up. I stopped doing those things for a while because it was in danger of becoming perceived as exactly that . . . 'Oh now I can go off and make a Volkswagen out of telephone directories' and so on. It wasn't about those things. It's why they ended so quickly and why the work tried to develop in other ways. It's not a joke about how many Irishmen does it take to change a light bulb – I should say a Scotsman – it's a much longer story than that and it never ends.

TM: How do you earn a living as an artist given the fact that most of your work is transient, it's built in a particular place, it's so large that it can't be bought or purchased or possessed and then it's disassembled, and reassembled in another form in another place?

DM: Well, the answer to that is that that's only some of the work we do. But when we do do that we're generally paid a performance fee.

TM: But do you feel a pressure to do small-scale works because they can be commodities that are easy to sell?

DM: Yes, but it was a lot worse when I was working with a gallery. That was very 'Give us stuff we can sell'. But I never really sensed it so clearly at the time: 'You make these lovely big installations but could you make us a couple of wee things that we could sell?' I sort of resisted that at the time because it interfered with what I was doing at first and my mind was naturally going off on this big scale installation work. Now, fortunately, I'm able to do both and I can always do the small ones to support the next big thing. Now whether that's a kind of business or whether that's also to do with the creative thing is a moot point. But I think if I were honest I'd say the two things are mixed.

TM: It seems that one of your interests has been, consistently, leaps in scale.

DM: Yes, I would say so. It's a way of refuting that typecasting thing again: 'Oh you're the guy who only builds things 100 feet tall and made out of 10,000 car tyres'. 'No. We also do things the size of your thumb, made out of 5,000 little individual pieces of copper wire' . . . 'So you're the guy who make those little things out of copper wire?' 'No. We also made the Trophy Room'. It's like not being pinned down at all. Why should you want to be pinned down?

TM: Are you an urban artist at heart though? I know some of the earliest work you made was in a rural context, the leaf carpets you made for the art school in Dundee, but since then it seems to me you've been fired up by the city and that's where most of your art has been made.

DM: That's interesting but I've never really thought about that to be honest. I'd like to think that if someone dumped me in a park, or by the seaside then I'd respond . . . but then maybe I'd still make something industrial somehow . . .

TM: There's no way now you'd ever conceive of making sculpture out of rocks, stones, leaves, grass . . .

DM: I wouldn't really write them off, no I wouldn't say that at all. I think that would be bad news to know I would never make sculpture out of rocks.

TM: Magicians tend to operate by sleight of hand. It seems you are almost an in-your-face magician. Things are transformed right up in front of your nose, in the public domain. Do you identify at all with that idea? Is there an element of the magician or the shaman in you?

DM: There is, but the only thing that upsets me about it is the phrase 'sleight of hand', because it always sounds as if you very easily pull the dog out of the hankie. And when we do it, and it is 'we' because it's me working with loads of assistants, with chains and harnesses, and anvils and welders and grinders and all the money that costs, it ain't a sleight of hand. There's an awful long way to go to produce this thing, whatever it is. Maybe in the end we tend to make things look as if they happened easily and I worry about that. Maybe I finish things off too much.

TM: How much of yourself do you give to a particular work? Obviously it takes up all your physical time and energy but do you ever feel that you've given part of your deeper self? . . . Some people might say that it's quite depersonalised, your work . . .

DM: Do you think so?

TM: No, but I want to know how much of yourself you give?

DM: I think it's heart and soul stuff. It's one of the things that makes it so exciting to me. It's one of the things that makes it so knackering. I give a lot and I'll get a kind of mystical thing happening half way through the job when I blend into the damn thing and it's almost a kind of hippy experience. I don't generally talk about it in terms like this, I generally keep this to myself, but there is such a mantra involved in most of my work, a repetitive thing, that will build up the level of energy involved, the level of energy needed to make the work that I actually fuse together with the thing, that's the oddest experience.

21

TM: What do you think is the most effective work you've made in the last fifteen years? In your own terms?

DM: I think the most effective work is the magazine pieces, the magazine installations, without a doubt. The response from these pieces is always superb, always really positive, always draws a big audience, always gets me talking to that big audience, always gets me more work. I love making them.

TM: The idea of staging is very strong in your work. You must have a sense of theatre and of drama?

DM: Absolutely. But it's theatre/drama performance. I'd liken it subtly to the very dry seventies performance, like Stuart Brisley, hard things, hard performance, some of that was really interesting, some of it was a load of old bollocks, unfortunately. But it actually continued on into the eighties and I was very much interested in that. I liked the idea of that because there's someone standing there watching you do it. You've got an audience which means you're not locked up in your studio doing this thing by yourself, like no-one even knows that you exist. So the drama is a definite ingredient because they're big, physical, dangerous looking theatrical pieces. There's another thing we have a problem with in this country: you make something you'd like to be funny, or theatrical, but in some circles of the art world that's a definite no-no, and I find that rather bizarre.

TM: Do you think humour is a strong weapon?

DM: It's a very strong weapon, the best that you've got. If you are going to be a preacher, someone along those lines, if you are going to get people to come and see this stuff, then it's got to be there. It's no good telling jokes about it, the humour has got to be part of the work. Although I must admit I find it a bit strange when I find people laughing in the same space as my work, people are always more weird than you imagine.

It's just the notion of using humour like that in this country, while it has this huge strength if you are a comedian or you write plays or a book or even a film, to use it in art somehow is not the right thing to do. It has more to do with the fact that people who think like that have their heads stuck up their own arse, not to put too fine a point on it.

TM: Are you saying we take art too seriously?

DM: No, no that's not what I'm saying at all. Art should be taken very seriously, humour and all. To me to put humour in it probably makes it more serious. But I think there are people who take certain things so seriously that they're humourless, unfortunately some of those guys are in charge.

TM: But isn't it themselves they're taking seriously rather than art?

DM: No . . . well, they do take themselves seriously, you're right. But art and artists may suffer because of that.

TM: Do you ever get inspired by art? I don't mean by your own art, I mean, does other people's art fuel your own art?

DM: Yes, but not directly. If inspiration is just a thing that makes you want to go off and do something then absolutely yes, I am inspired by other people's art and also by films, books, music and things like that. I won't run off a watercolour of the seaside, though, or carve a piece of wood, the inspiration manifests itself in other ways.

TM: I'm thinking of the reclining figure or reclining nude, the only pieces I can think of off the top of my head where you've directly referred to art and artworks.

DM: No, I think there are references in every single piece. It's impossible to get away from that. I don't think it's something you have to hide at all, in fact references are probably best celebrated, you are after all talking about the roots of your idea. My work does refer to art rather a lot but also films and performance. If I'm honest I would say I looked for something raunchy to refer to, if not downright sexy, then definitely raunchy. I can't help myself doing that. I might, therefore, look more at contemporary film and music than contemporary art. There's not enough raunchiness in contemporary art in my opinion.

TM: Are you interested in virtual reality?

DM: Not at all. Total reality. Virtual reality – what a nonsensical phrase, what a stupid thing to say! Virtual reality! Doesn't make any sense to me at all! I worry about stuff like that. If that's the thing that's going to be developed in the next few years then that's bad news for everybody.

TM: So there's no substitute for experiencing one of your sculptures? You can't develop it on a computer as a concept?

DM: I think there's no substitute for experience of anything first-hand.

TM: Do you have an idea of the mother of all David Mach projects that can't quite be realised at the moment because sponsorship isn't there? I was thinking of a parallel with, say, Christo's wanting to cover the Reichstag, which is finally happening but has taken years. Is there this mythical project in your mind?

DM: Well, I was asked to work up some proposals for the M8 motorway between Glasgow and Edinburgh. My proposal was to build a series of pyramids, squares really, they had three corners of each square sticking out of the ground, because I didn't just want to build an Egyptian pyramid the same way I didn't want to build a Greek temple. They were designed to be made out of thousands of sea containers, used as building blocks. It's quite possible to build these things but it takes a lot of money.

TM: And they'd be bigger than the pyramids in Egypt?

DM: Yes. They'd be much bigger than that. The whole proposal got a bit out of hand in my head so that it became a kind of master plan for the whole of the M8, so that this road between Edinburgh and Glasgow became an incredible art corridor like Monument Valley or the Valley of the Kings except, of course, it is in Lanarkshire mainly so the weather would be crap. But the proposal turned into five main sculptures and a whole backup package of hotels, leisure complexes and so on. The biggest sculpture was the Tartan Army; 10,000 concrete, steel and fibreglass figures, in positions of movement, running, brandishing swords and so on, 10 feet tall, marching across acres of fields and through a man-made loch. Each figure would have individual features and would be highly colourfully painted with individual tartans picked out. I imagine all sorts of things happening in the form of sponsorship: Americans paying for a complete figure to be made with their face, a kind of portraiture and then you could have a big Sean Connery at the head of the army, except, of course, he wouldn't have to pay . . . I'd love to do it. It would change the whole economy of that area of Scotland, in fact it would double the tourist industry for the whole country. It would provide a lot of jobs for a lot of years. I'm perfectly serious about making these things. I know people are interested and I may actually get to forge ahead and build something like this. Who knows? The Tartan Army – there's an idea for the next millennium.

TM: Are you a patriot at all?

DM: I try not to be nationalistic but I do find myself laughing when England get thrashed at cricket. I don't want to be a professional Scot, I don't like that. I'm very hard on Scotland. I want it to be the most open-minded nation in the world, no racism, equal opportunities, great ideas, that kind of stuff. I know it's not like that and when I see evidence of it it pisses me off.

TM: Do you feel a strong cultural identity with Scotland or Britain in general?

DM: With Britain in general, Scotland in particular. My dad's Polish, we were brought up travelling regularly to Poland on holidays and I feel that's had a big influence on how I'm shaped, and my father's had a big influence on me. But he's not Scottish, absolutely not, he still talks with quite a thick accent. His experience, his background, where he comes from is very different.

TM: Do you have to have a big ego to make big art?

DM: I'd like to think it wasn't bigger than anyone else's. That's one thing my folks taught me – feed your ego, get satisfaction from what you do. My dad worked down the pit for thirty-six years, a tough, dangerous job. When he was a kid he worked in the mines of Siberia. My brother and I were always told that we'd never go down the pit. Thank God, you know. It's not a job I could have handled, I would have been scared all the time. The point is, to my dad he wasn't doing a silly job, it wasn't manual labour. He loved being a miner, it was a profession, a vocation almost. I never really saw him pissed off, he was always pretty happy about things, he fed his ego off being a man, being a miner, providing a living for himself and his family. He gleaned everything out of that, he got satisfaction from what he did without being an egomaniac.

TM: Do you ever think that art is futile? When you talk about your father, passionately, the mines have now been closed down. Did you ever think, two or three years ago, why the hell am I making art when this is happening?

DM: Yes, I do think that. But then I have to remind myself that art is incredibly important. Without art, cultures die, mines close, bridges collapse, rivers dry up. I mean it, I think having art, having practising artists, and I mean contemporary artists, not paintings of flowers, not decorations, is important to our survival and has a direct impact on it. Without artists and their ideas nothing flourishes, nothing changes, nothing grows. It's not futile, it can have a huge impact. I bet the first guy to invent the wheel wasn't inventing the wheel at all, I bet he was just some artist playing around with a bit of stone. Maybe he was a caveman, maybe he was carving this stone with a bit of flint and this thing broke off and rolled down the hill. There were two guys there to witness this, one of them wanted to beat the shit out of him for being such a smart arse, the other guy broke into a cold sweat when he realised the potential for this new 'invention'. The rest is history.

TM: Do you think art can change the way people see the world?

DM: Yes. I think it can change an awful lot of things. I think it has. I think that's been proved, countless times over the centuries. Otherwise they'd have bulldozed the pyramids down. If I didn't believe it I wouldn't be doing it.

Tim Marlow is Editor of tate The art magazine *and is a regular presenter of* Kaleidoscope *on Radio 4.*

23

FUEL FOR THE FIRE
RIVERSIDE STUDIOS, LONDON, AUGUST 1986

ADDING FUEL TO THE FIRE
METRONOM GALLERY, BARCELONA, JUNE 1987

OUTSIDE IN
SCOTTISH NATIONAL GALLERY OF MODERN ART, EDINBURGH, AUGUST 1987

NATURAL CAUSES
WIENER SECESSION, VIENNA, SEPTEMBER 1987

UNTITLED
DUNLOP GALLERY, REGINA (CANADA), APRIL 1988

A MILLION MILES AWAY

SIGNS OF LIFE
PROVINCIAAL MUSEUM, HASSELT (BELGIUM), MAY 1988

THE ART THAT CAME APART

MUSÉE D'ART CONTEMPORAIN, MONTREAL, SEPTEMBER 1988

PLOUGHMAN'S LUNCH
MIDDLETON HALL, MILTON KEYNES, JUNE 1989

HERE TO STAY
TRAMWAY, GLASGOW, MARCH 1990

LIKE A VIRGIN . . .
UJAZDOWSKI CASTLE CENTRE FOR CONTEMPORARY ART, WARSAW, MARCH 1993

GOING DOWN
VIAFARINI, MILAN, MAY 1993

FLAYED, STRETCHED AND TANNED
WALSALL ARTGALLERY WEST MIDLANDS DECEMBER 1993

FULLY FURNISHED

MUSEUM OF CONTEMPORARY ART, SAN DIEGO, JANUARY 1994

UNTITLED
MUSÉE LÉON DIERX, RÉUNION ISLAND, MARCH 1994

WHITE WATER, YELLOW SPLASH, RED DASH
NEWLYN ART GALLERY, CORNWALL, MAY 1994

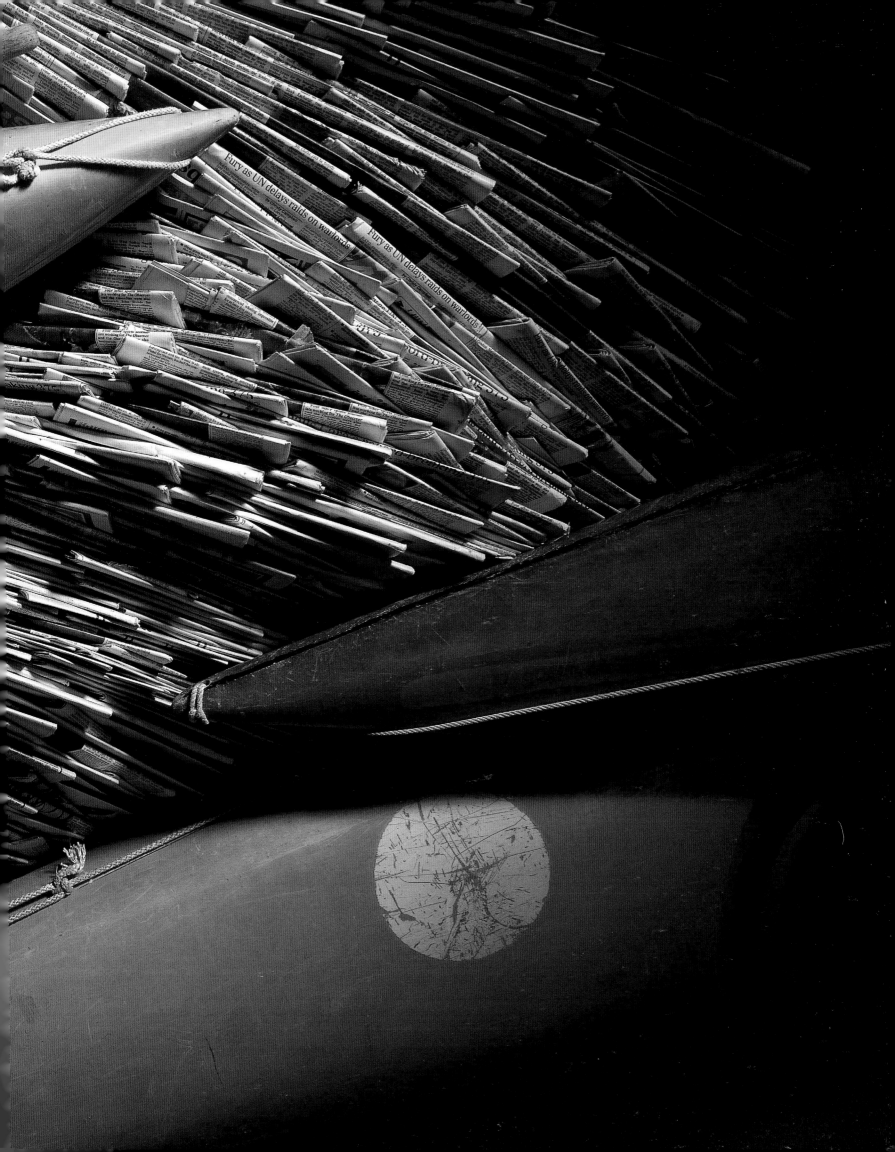

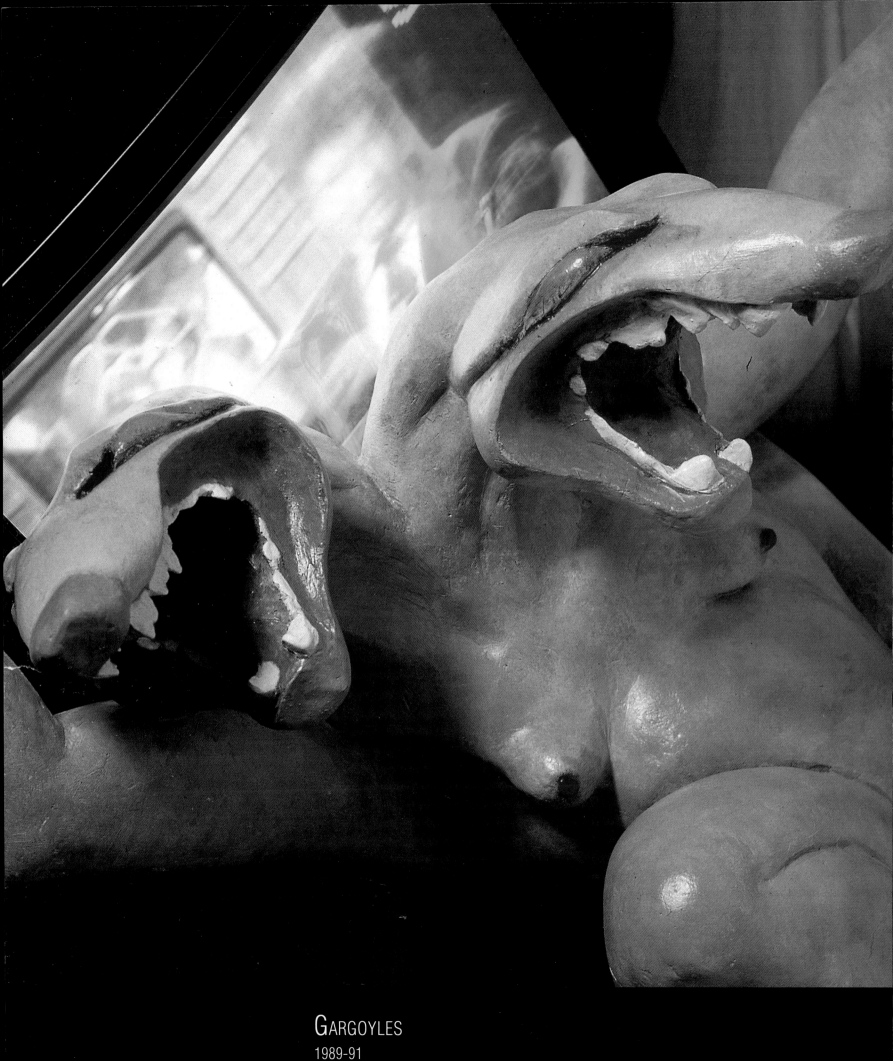

GARGOYLES

1989-91

A HUNDRED AND ONE DALMATIONS

CALL OF THE WILD

1991

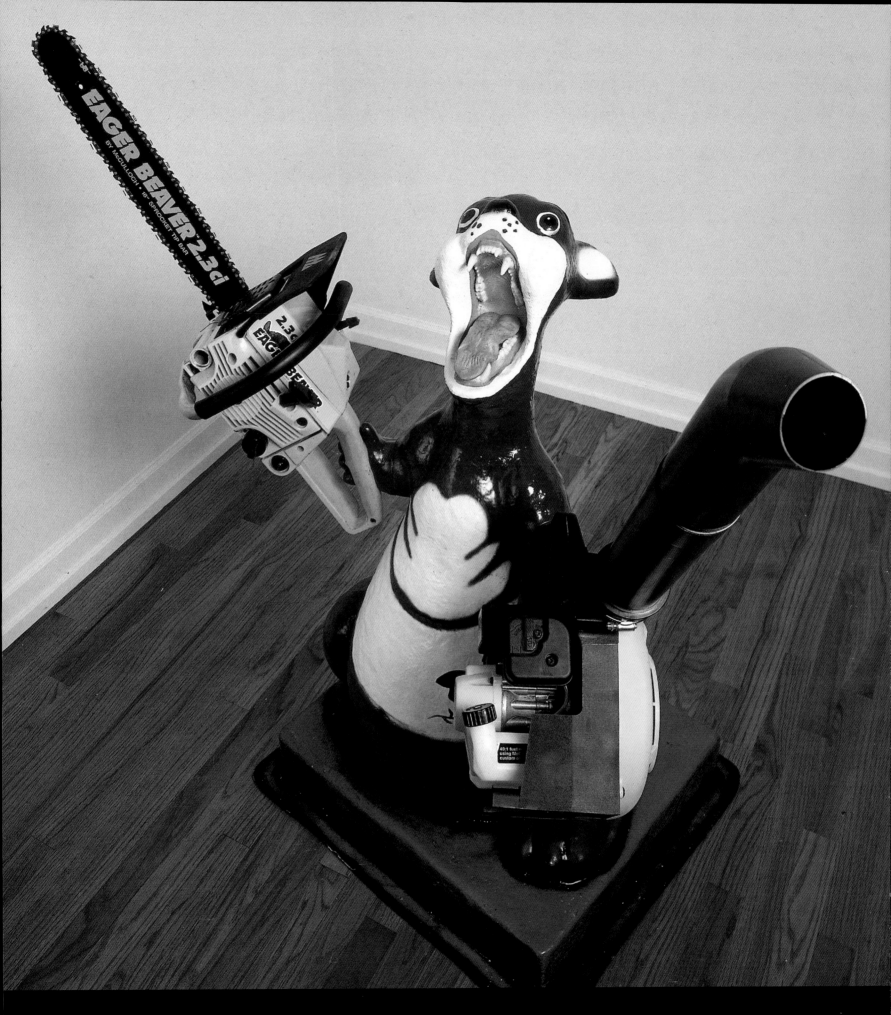

CALL OF THE WILD, THIS TIME IT'S REVENGE
1991

DON'T GIVE A FUCK BEARS
1991-92

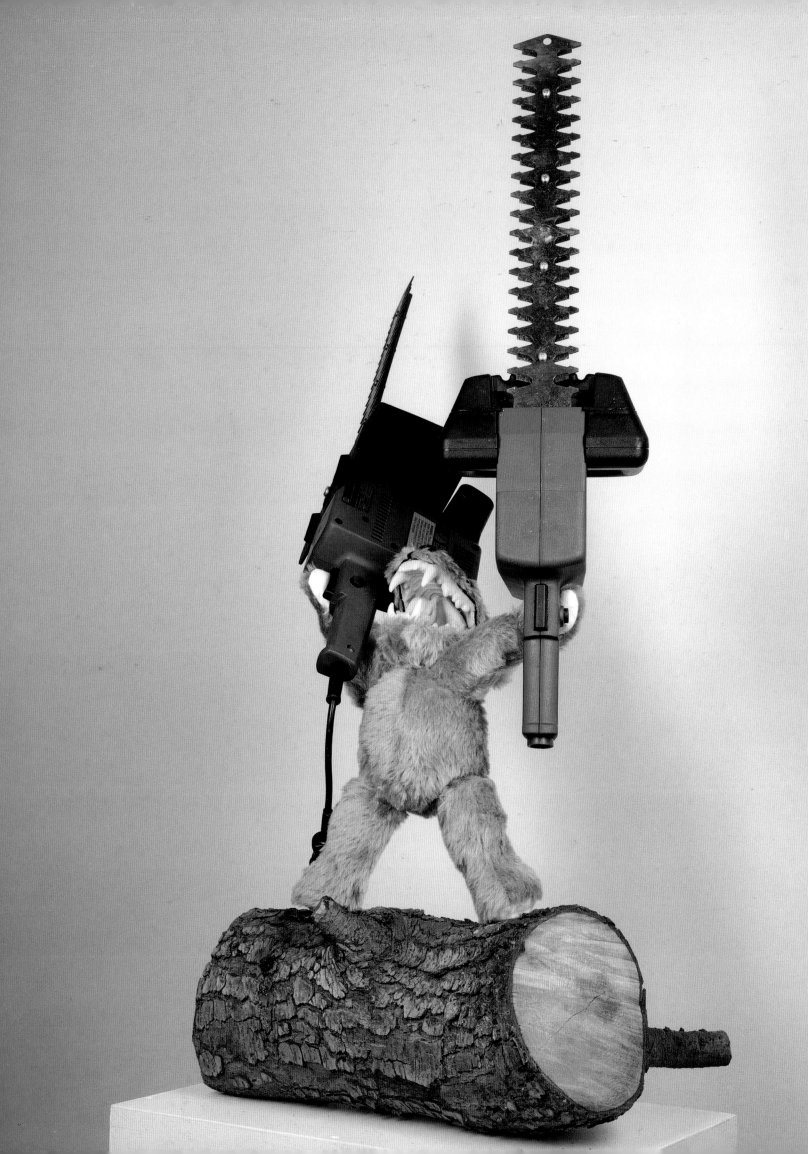

TROPHIES

King of the Road, 1990 (detail)

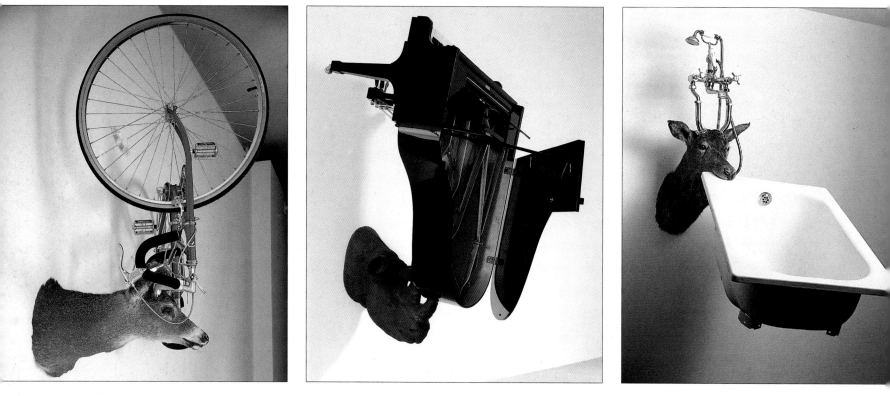

The Bike Stops Here, 1989
Nicely out of Tune, 1990
All Mod Cons, 1990

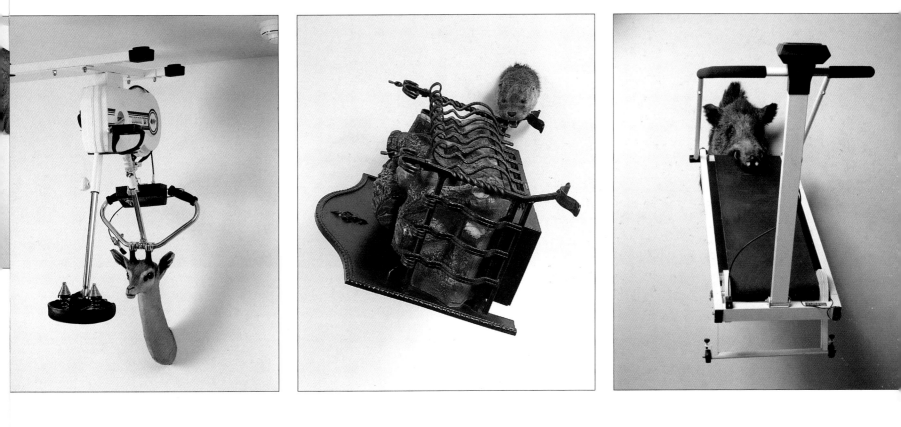

Fit for Life, 1990
Mistaken Identity, 1990
Walk on the Wild Side, 1990

THE TROPHY ROOM
UJAZDOWSKI CASTLE CENTRE FOR CONTEMPORARY ART, WARSAW, MARCH 1993

HEAVENLY PURSUITS
GALERIE NIKKI DIANA MARQUARDT, PARIS, MAY 1992

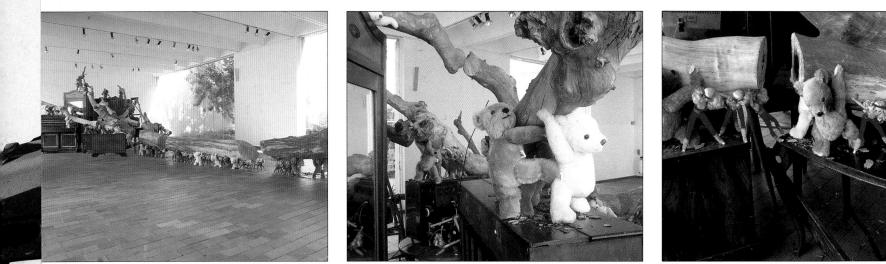

IF YOU GO DOWN TO THE WOODS TODAY
FUNDACIÓ JOAN MIRÓ, BARCELONA, JUNE 1987

No Rest for the Wicked
GALERIE ANDATA/RITORNO, GENEVA, NOVEMBER 1988

MATCH HEADS

1992-1994

ALL ROUND THE HOUSES
UNION DES BANQUES SUISSES, GENEVA, AUGUST 1993

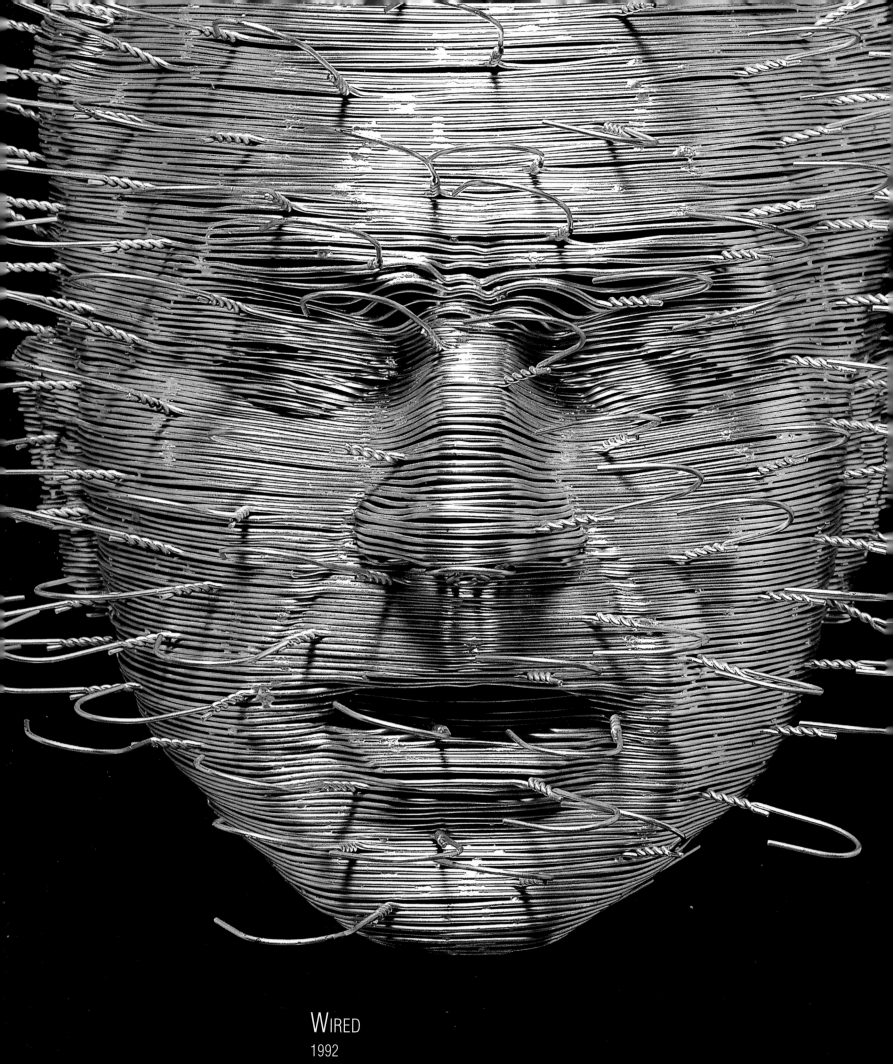

WIRED
1992

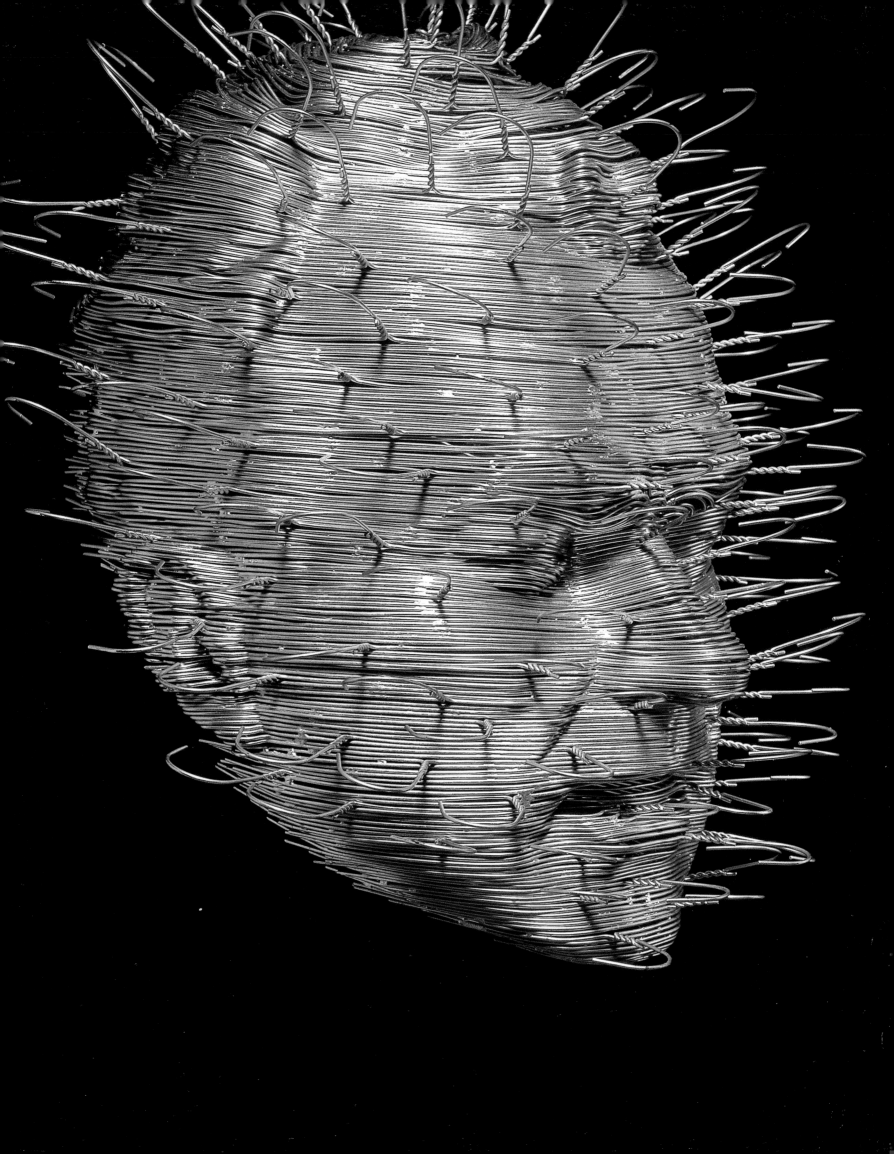

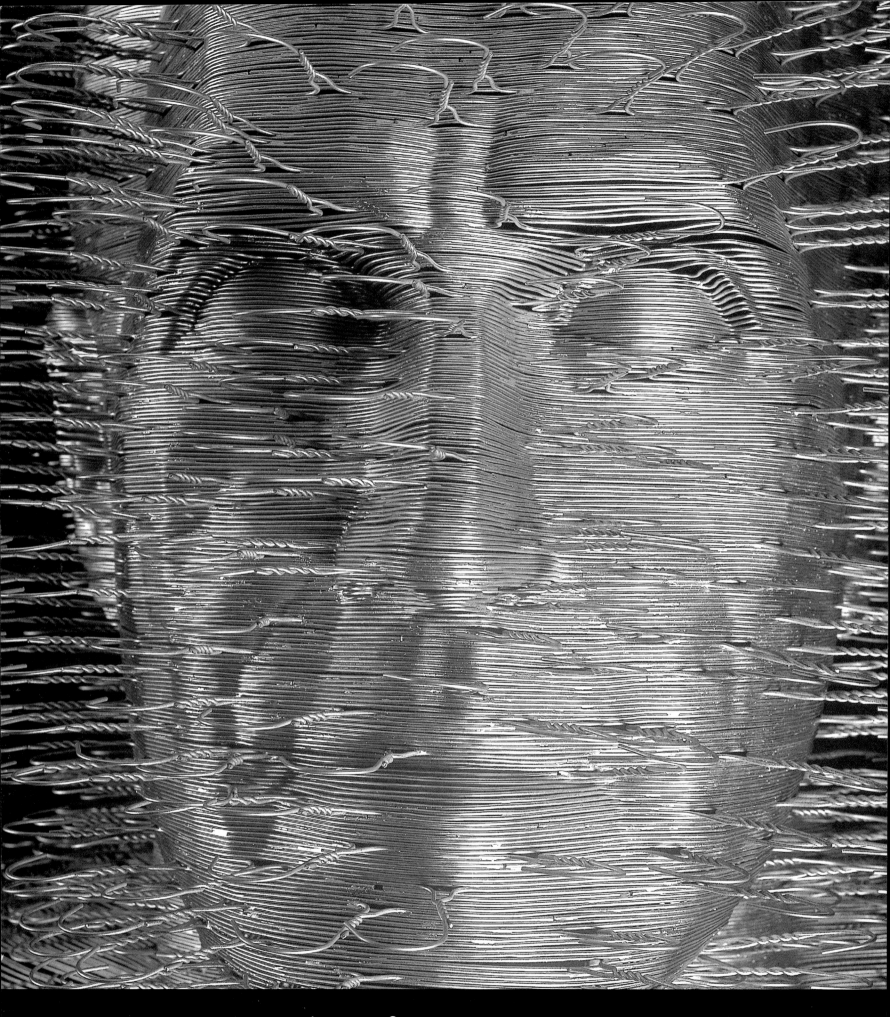

LIKENESS GUARANTEED

NEWLYN ART GALLERY, CORNWALL, MAY 1994

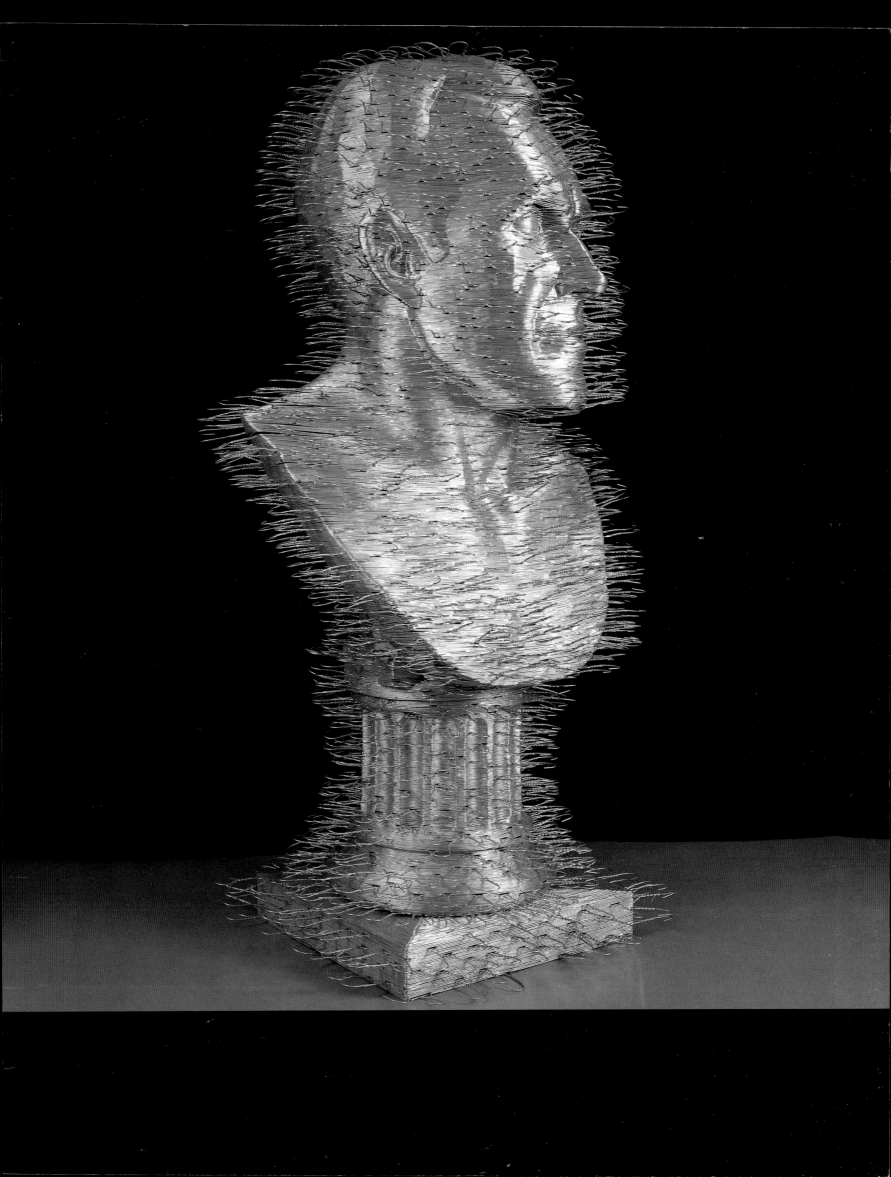

TEMPLE AT TYRE
LEITH DOCKS, EDINBURGH, NOVEMBER 1994

It Takes Two
KING STREET, GLASGOW, 1994

TARTAN ARMY
PROPOSALS FOR THE M8 CORRIDOR, 1994

DARLINGTON SCULPTURE PROPOSAL
TO BE EXECUTED IN 1995

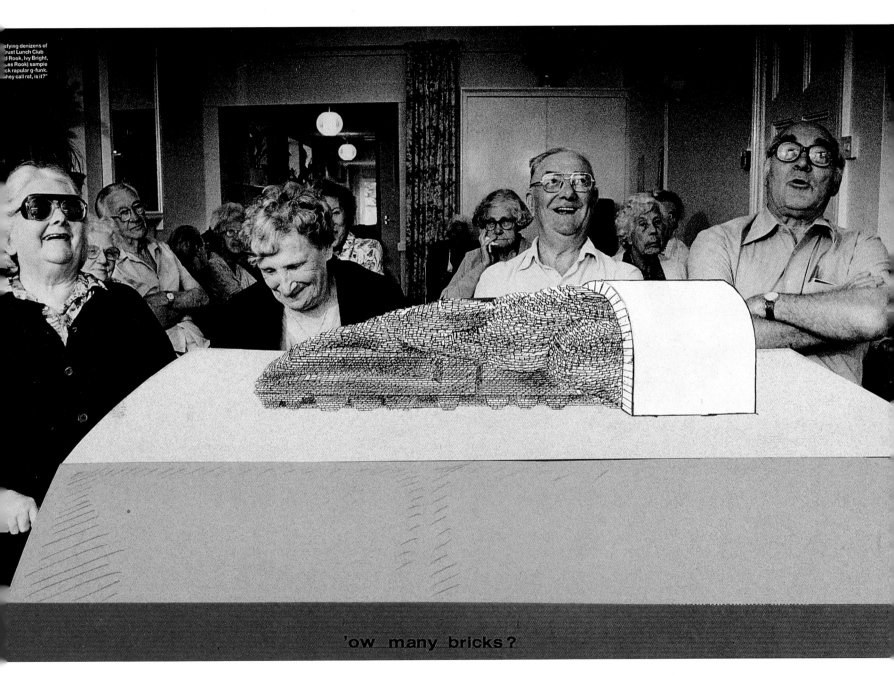

BIOGRAPHY
EXHIBITIONS
TELEVISION
BIBLIOGRAPHY

BIOGRAPHY

1956	Born in Methil, Fife (Scotland)
1974-1979	Duncan Jordanstone College of Art, Dundee
1975	Pat Holmes Memorial Prize
1976	Duncan of Drumfork Travelling Scholarship
1977	SED Minor Travelling Scholarship
1978	SED Major Travelling Scholarship
1979-1982	Royal College of Art, London
1982	RCA Drawing Prize
1988	Nominated for Turner Prize, Tate Gallery, London
1992	Won Lord Provost's Prize, RGI, Glasgow

SOLO EXHIBITIONS

1981
March	Richard Booth Bookshop, Hay-on-Wye (Wales)

1982
Aug-Sept	Lisson Gallery, London
Nov	New 57 Gallery, Edinburgh
Dec-Jan	Galerie t'Venster, Rotterdam

1983
Jan	Mock Shop, Kingston Polytechnic, London
Sept-Oct	'Castaways', Galerie Andata/Ritorno, Geneva
Nov-Dec	Ateliers Contemporains d'Arts Plastiques, St Brieuc (France)

1985
Feb-April	'Towards a Landscape', Museum of Modern Art, Oxford
Oct-Nov	Galerie Foksal, Warsaw
Dec	Stoke City Museum, Stoke-on-Trent

1986
Jan	Cleveland Art Gallery, Middlesborough
April	'David Mach Roadshow', Barbara Toll Fine Art, New York
April-May	Mercer Union Gallery, Toronto
June-Aug	Herning Kunstmuseum, Herning (Denmark)
Aug	'Fuel for the Fire', Riverside Studios, London
Aug-Sept	Seagate Gallery, Dundee
Sept-Oct	'If you go Down to the Woods', Corner House, Manchester
Sept-Oct	'Chimney Sweep', Town Hall, Manchester
Nov	Sherratt & Hughes Bookshop, Leadenhall Market, London
Dec	National Museum of Photography, Film & Television, Bradford
Dec-Jan	Hacienda Club, Manchester

1987
May	Musée des Arts Decoratifs, Centre du Verre, Paris
June-July	'Si avui t'endinses en els boscos', Fundació Joan Miró, Barcelona
June-Sept	'Adding Fuel to the Fire', Metronom Gallery, Barcelona
Aug	Mosaic, permanently sited in Cattle Market Car Park, Kingston upon Thames, London
Sept-Oct	'Natural Causes', Wiener Secession, Vienna
Oct-Dec	One of two British representatives at the 19th Biennale, Sao Paolo
Dec	'Chinese Whispers', Nicola Jacobs Gallery, London

1988
March-June	'A Hundred and One Dalmations', Tate Gallery, London
April-May	Dunlop Art Gallery, Regina, Saskatchewan (Canada)
May-June	'A Million Miles Away', Barbara Toll Fine Art, New York
May-Nov	'Signs of Life', Provinciaal Museum, Hasselt (Belgium)
May	'Multi-Story, Car Park', BBC Television Centre, London
Aug	'A Nice Location', Kawasaki City Museum, Tokyo
Sept-Jan	'The Art That Came Apart', Musée d'Art Contemporain, Montreal
Oct-Dec	'David Mach', Galerie Ek'Ymose 1, Bordeaux
Nov-Dec	'Parvis 2', Tarbes (France)
Nov-Dec	Galerie Andata/Ritorno, Geneva

1989
Jan-Feb	'Scream of Consciousness', Artspace, San Francisco
Jan-March	'David Mach', FGG Gallery, Frankfurt
Feb-April	'Tamed, Trained and Framed', Maurice Keitelman Gallery, Brussels
June-Aug	'Liberté, Egalité, Fraternité – A New Utopia', Galerie Nikki Diana Marquardt, Paris
June	'Ploughman's Lunch', Middleton Hall, Milton Keynes
Aug	'Kissin' Cousins', Hamburg Messe, Hamburg
Sept-Oct	'Along Classical Lines', Melbourne Spoleto Festival, National Gallery of Victoria, Melbourne
Oct-Nov	'Home Cookin'', Galerie 175, Brussels
Oct-Nov	'Wet and Dry', Cultural Centre, Madrid

Dec-Jan	'Five Easy Pieces', Barbara Toll Fine Art, New York
Dec-March	'A Hair's Breadth', Brooklyn Museum, New York
Dec	Installed *Out of Order*, a permanent piece commissioned by the Royal Borough of Kingston upon Thames, London

1990
March-April	'Here to Stay', Tramway, Glasgow
May	'Chicago Trophies', Chicago Art Fair, Chicago
June-July	'Over to the Right a Bit', House of Ukrainian Artists, Kiev
Oct-Nov	'Creature Comforts', Pittsburgh Center for the Arts, Pittsburgh

1991
April-Aug	'David Mach: Sculpture', Ace Contemporary Art, Los Angeles
May-Aug	'David Mach: Sculpture', Maurice Keitelman Gallery, Brussels
July	Gallery 400, University of Illinois, Chicago
Oct-April	'It Takes Two', sculpture commissioned by Camden Arts and British Rail, Euston Square Gardens, London

1992
Jan-Feb	Orpheus Gallery, Belfast
March-April	Barbara Toll Fine Art, New York
May-Aug	'Welcome to Euromach', Galerie Nikki Diana Marquardt, Paris

1993
March-May	'David Mach: Sculpture', Ujazdowski Castle Centre for Contemporary Art, Warsaw
April-June	'Between the Lines', Hakone Open-Air Museum (Japan)
May-Sept	'David Mach: New Work', Viafarini, Milan
May-Sept	'David Mach: New Work', Studio Casoli, Milan
Aug	Installed a commissioned sculpture in new headquarters of Union des Banques Suisses, Geneva
Sept-Oct	'Square Town/Town Square', Seagate Gallery, Dundee
Sept-Oct	'Match Heads', the Gallery, Essex University, Colchester
Dec-Jan	'Flayed, Stretched and Tanned', Walsall Art Gallery, Walsall

1994
Jan-April	'Fully Furnished', Museum of Contemporary Art, San Diego

March-June	'Freeze', Musée León Dierx, Réunion Island
April-May	Drawings, CASK, Kitakyushu (Japan)
April-May	'Hako', Glasgow Print Studio, Glasgow
May-June	'Likeness Guaranteed', Newlyn Art Gallery, Cornwall
July-Aug	'Headcase', Aberdeen Art Gallery, Aberdeen
Aug-Sept	Sculpture installation in the Sun Pavilion, Harrogate
Sept	Installed four commissioned collages in headquarters of Union des Banques Suisses, Geneva
Nov-Dec	*Temple at Tyre*, Leith Docks, Edinburgh
Dec	'David Mach', Mercer Art Gallery, Harrogate

GROUP EXHIBITIONS
1982

Feb-March	Hildebrandtstrasse, Düsseldorf
July-Aug	'Sculpture at the Open Air Theatre', Regent's Park, London
Oct-Nov	'London/New York', Lisson Gallery, London

1983

Jan-March	'Truc et Troc, Leçons des Choses', ARC, Paris
April-May	'Young Blood', Riverside Studios, London
May-June	'Beelden/Sculpture', Lijnbaancentrum, Rotterdam
May-Sept	'Nécessités', Château de la Roche Jagu, Brittany
July	'Danse à Aix', Aix-en-Provence
July-Sept	'Diagonale', Espace Montevideo, Antwerp
Aug-Sept	'British Sculpture 83', Hayward Gallery, London
Aug-Sept	'Sculptors' Drawings', Air Gallery, London
Oct	'Sculpture Symposium', Yorkshire Sculpture Park
Oct-Dec	'Ars 83', Ateneum Museum, Helsinki
Nov	'Art Ink 83', ICA, London

1984

Feb	'New Directions', Cleveland Art Gallery, Middlesborough
March	'Plus Value', Galerie Eric Fabre, Paris
March	'Acquisitions', Fond Régional Art Contemporain du Rhônes-Alpes (France)
May-Oct	International Garden Festival, Liverpool

June	'Art Within Reach', Air Gallery, London
July-Sept	'Paper Trails', Bluecoat Gallery, Liverpool
Aug-Sept	'Repeats', Coracle Press, London
Aug	'Demarcation', Edinburgh International Festival, Edinburgh
Sept	'Festival à la Bastion', Geneva
Sept	'Art on the Map', Canterbury Fringe Festival, Canterbury
Oct	'L'Hôtel Revisité' (presented by Fondation Charles Jourdan), Avenue de New York, Paris
Nov-Dec	'Low-Tech', Coracle Press at Rees Martin Art Services, London

1985

Feb-March	'Still Life', Barbara Toll Fine Art, New York
May	'Royal Scotsman' (production and exhibition of work on board the *Royal Scotsman*), Edinburgh
May-Sept	'Beelden op de Berg', Wageningen (The Netherlands)
June	'The Interim Art Wall, Ceiling, Floor Show' with Artangel Roadshow, London
June-Oct	'Automobiennale', Middelheim Museum, Antwerp
June-Dec	'David Mach, Colin Nicholas', London Business School, London
Sept	Canterbury Fringe Festival
Oct	'Impulse', Galerie Loehrl, Mönchengladbach (Germany)
All year	Scottish Travelling Drawing Show
All year	FRAC du Rhônes-Alpes touring exhibition in France

1986

April	'Conversations', Germans van Eck Gallery, New York
May	'Sculpture in the City', Bath
May	International Contemporary Art Fair, London
May-July	'Spring Fling', Edinburgh
June-Oct	International Garden Festival, Stoke-on-Trent
July-Aug	Batley Art Gallery, Huddersfield
Aug-Sept	'Painting and Sculpture Today: 1986', Indianapolis Museum of Art, Indiana
Oct	'Contrariwise', Glyn Vivian Art Gallery, Swansea

1987

| Jan | '2D/3D', The Laing Art Gallery, Newcastle upon Tyne |
| Jan-Feb | Sutton College of Further Education, Sutton Coldfield, West Midlands |

March	Idsall School, Shifnal, Shropshire
April-May	City Artists Gallery, London
May-June	'The British Edge', ICA, Boston
May-June	'Stichting Art Paper 87', Jan Van Eyck Akademie, Maastricht
July	'Zomerfestyn 87', Amsterdam
Aug	'Black and White', Nicola Jacobs Gallery, London
Aug-Oct	'Century 87', Amsterdam
Aug-Oct	'The Vigorous Imagination', Scottish National Gallery of Modern Art, Edinburgh
Sept-Oct	'Metal and Motion', Brighton
Sept-Oct	'The Vessel', Serpentine Gallery, London
Oct	'International Iron Sculpture Symposium', Kitakyushu (Japan)

1988

Feb-March	'Off the Beaten Track', UK/LA Festival, UCLA, Los Angeles
Feb-March	'New Directions: New Attitudes in Scottish Art' touring exhibition in Yugoslavia
May	'New British Art', Tate Gallery, Liverpool
June-July	'Wakefield 100', Wakefield
July	Henley Arts Festival, Henley-on-Thames
Sept-Jan	British Arts Retrospective, touring exhibition in France

1989

Feb-March	Opening exhibition, Barbizon Gallery, Glasgow
June-Aug	'Scottish Art Since 1990', National Gallery of Modern Art, Edinburgh
July	'Contemporary British Art', Hammond Galleries, Lancaster, Ohio
Aug-Sept	Summer Exhibition, Royal Academy of Art, London

1990

Jan-Feb	'Guillaume Bijl, David Mach, Carmen Perrin', Galerie Andata/Ritorno, Geneva
Feb-March	'Scottish Art Since 1900', Scottish Gallery, London
Feb-March	'Scottish Art Since 1900', Barbican, London
May-Sept	National Garden Festival, Gateshead
May-Sept	'Three Scottish Sculptors', Venice Biennale, Venice
June-Aug	'Die Collectie Alsnoch', Provinciaal Museum, Hasselt (Belgium)
July-Aug	'Sculptors Work on Paper', Flowers East, London

July-Nov   'New Purchases', Museum of
Contemporary Art, Antwerp,
Belgium

Aug-
June 1991   'British Art Now: A Subjective
View', touring exhibition in Japan
visiting Setagaya Museum, Tokyo,
Fukuoka Art Museum, Nagoya
City Art Museum, Tochigi Prefec-
tural Museum of Fine Arts, Hyogo
Prefectural Museum of Modern
Art, and Hiroshima City Museum
of Contemporary Art

1991
March-April   'Guillaume Bijl, Marcel Duchamp,
David Mach, Jurg Moser, Carmen
Perrin', Galerie Moi-Farine,
Geneva

May   William Jackson Gallery, London

June-Aug   Summer Exhibition, Royal
Academy of Art, London

June-Aug   'Kunst Europa', Karlsruhe
(Germany)

June-Aug   'Selected Artists', Galerie Nikki
Marquardt, Paris

July-Sept   'Virtue and Vision: Sculpture and
Scotland 1540-1990', Royal
Scottish Academy, Edinburgh

Aug-Sept   'Espace', Sculptors' Society of
Ireland, Dublin

Nov   'Sculpture and Sculptors'
Drawings', William Jackson
Gallery, London

1992
Jan-Feb   'Challenging Perspectives', Ash
Gallery, Edinburgh

June   Installation, De Werf, Aalst
(Belgium)

June   New Purchases, National Art
Collections Fund, Sothebys,
London

June-July   Annual Sculpture Exhibition,
Millfield School, Somerset

June-Aug   Sculpture Biennale, Jesus
College, Cambridge

Sept   'Critic's Choice', Cooling Gallery,
London

Nov   'Decade Show', Duncan
Jordanstone College of Art, City
Museum and Art Galleries and
various sites around Dundee

Dec   'The Selected Line', William
Jackson Gallery, London

1993
March-April   'Vormin Herhaling', Jansen &
Kooy, Amsterdam

May-June   'Summer Seen', William Jackson
Gallery, London

Sept-Jan   Sculpture Garden, Lewisham town
centre, London

1994
June-Sept   'British Sculpture', Beaux Arts,
London

July-Sept   'Summer Show', William Jackson
Gallery, London

Oct   'A Changing World: Fifty Years of
Sculpture from the British Council
Collection', The State Russian
Museum, St Petersburg

Dec   Absolut exhibition, Royal Academy
of Art, London

TELEVISION
1983
Jan   *Alter Image* series, Channel 4. Made a reclining figure piece for the first programme.

1984
Aug   *Newsnight*, BBC2. Ten minute documentary
film as part of Edinburgh Festival coverage,
comprising mainly background information
on Mach and concentrating on his piece in
the 'Demarcation' exhibition.

1985
Sept   *Saturday Review*, BBC1. Film of some of
the early match heads being burnt at the
Canterbury Fringe Festival and an interview.

1988
May   *Mach I, Mach II, Mach III, Mach IV*, BBC1.
Five or ten minute sequences charting the
progress of Mach's installation 'Multi-Story,
Car Park' in the BBC Television Centre car
park to illustrate and advertise the BBC's
'British Art Week' programmes.

1990
Feb   *What the Papers Say*, BBC2. Mach created
a maze from 40 tons of newspapers which
was filmed for the title sequence.

April   *Clydeside Classic*, video scripted by Mach
and filmed as part of the *19.4.90 Television
Interventions* series shown at the Worldwide
Video Festival in Holland in October 1990;
at the Festival du Nouveau Cinema et de La
Video in Montreal in October 1990 and the
Australian International Video Festival in
November 1990.

1991
Jan   *Vanity Fair* commercial. Mach made a large
magazine sculpture for film commercial
shown both on television and cinema to
advertise the British launch of the magazine.

May   *The Late Show*, BBC2. One of the guest art
critics of the month.

1993
Feb   *The Love Weekend*, Channel 4. Made
condom sculpture.

May   *The Late Show*, BBC2. A 20 minute version
of the film *From Hill to Castle*, produced by
Annalogue Productions for BBC Scotland
and the Arts Council of Great Britain. This
showed the organisation and realisation of
the Ujazdowski Castle Exhibition.

July   *Off the Wall* series, BBC2. Made tyre
Parthenon with Byker Estate residents in
Newcastle.

1994
Jan   *The Great British Quiz*, BBC 1. Designed
and made the set for this series.

BIBLIOGRAPHY
David Mach: Master Builder, essay by Tom
Bendhem, Galerie t'Venster (Rotterdam) 1982

David Mach: Towards a Landscape, essay by
Marco Livingstone, Museum of Modern Art (Oxford) 1985.

David Mach: Fuel for the Fire, introduction by Mel
Gooding, Riverside Studios (London) 1986.

David Mach: Natural Causes, Weiner Secession
(Vienna) 1987.

A Hundred and One Dalmations, Tate Gallery
(London) 1988.

Secco y Mojado: Wet and Dry, Centro Cultural de
la Villa and the British Council (Madrid) 1989.

ArT RANDOM: David Mach, Marco Livingstone
(ed), Kyoto Shoin International Co Ltd (Kyoto,
Japan) 1990 (reprinted 1991).

*David Mach Magazine Installation: Between the
Lines*, Hakone Open-air Museum (Hakone-machi,
Japan) 1993.

David Mach: Temple at Tyre, Edinburgh District
Council (Edinburgh) 1995.

David Mach at the Zamak Ujazdowski, essay by
David Cassidy, Lampoon House Nasanori Omai
(Tokyo) 1995.